THE

OLYMPIC
ODYSSEY

THE
OLYMPIC
ODYSSEY

Rekindling the True Spirit of the Great Games

PHIL COUSINEAU

Quest Books
Theosophical Publishing House

Wheaton, Illinois ♦ Chennai (Madras), India

The Theosophical Society acknowledges with gratitude the generous support of the Kern Foundation for the publication of this book.

The Theosophical Publishing House
P. O. Box 270
Wheaton, IL 60189-0270

Cover art, book design, and typesetting by Dan Doolin

Photo Credits: The following images appear by the courtesy of the following sources:

Page xii: © copyright Gianni Dagli Orti/CORBIS
Page 20: © copyright The British Museum
Page 29: © copyright The Vatican Museum
Page 82: © copyright Michael Holford
Page 102: © copyright Araldo de Luca/CORBIS
Page 153: © copyright Bettman/CORBIS
Pages 14, 49, 55, 68, 70, 72, 119, 126, 148, 156, 171, 189, 201, 239: © copyright IOC/Olympic Museum Collections
Page 197: Source unknown

Every effort has been made to secure permission to reproduce the images in this book. Additional copyright holders are invited to contact the publisher so that proper credit can be given in future editions.

Library of Congress Cataloging-in-Publication Data

Cousineau, Phil.
The Olympic odyssey: rekindling the true spirit of
the great games / Phil Cousineau.—1st Quest ed.
p.   cm.
Includes bibliographical references and index.
ISBN 0-8356-0833-6
1. Olympics—Philosophy.   I. Title.

GV721.6.C69 2003
796.48—dc21   2003047175

6   5   4   3   2   1   *   03   04   05   06   07   08

Printed in the United States of America

*For the love of the games and
to all the guys down at Forest Park and at The Gym:
Biff, Tim, Mark, Ernie, Dennis, Frank, Bob, Steve,
Larry, Bob, Doug, Les, Ryan, Dwight, Cip, Dan,
Jack, Mac, Ronnie, Chuck,
and my brother
Paul*

CONTENTS

ACKNOWLEDGMENTS

✳

On a true odyssey, no one can go it alone. The odyssey of this book has been no exception. As wayward travelers customarily do, I would like to express my gratitude to all those who have helped me find my way home.

First, I wish to express my deep gratitude to my editor at Quest Books, Sharron Dorr, whose phone call about expanding a previous essay of mine on "The Myth of Sports" led me on this adventure. Her ardent belief in the transcendent, spiritual dimension of the Olympics and her faith in my ability to evoke it was a constant source of inspiration. In the spirit of the philosopher coach, she encouraged me to pursue excellence in my writing of the book in a way that would reflect the ancient code of excellence at the heart of the Great Games.

I also wish to express my deep appreciation to Carolyn Bond, whose truly Olympian editorial work helped me pick up the pace and clarify the book's vision. Thanks, too, to Nicole Krier, for her spirited support in marketing, and to Dan Doolin, for his resourcefulness in tracking down so many rich illustrations and for designing such a beautiful book.

My gratitude also goes to those who were gracious enough to consent to interviews—including Sarunas Marciulionis, Stuart Brown, Bruce Bochte, Steve Glass, Huston Smith, and Valerie Andrews—as well as to Matt Biondi, for helpful conversations several years ago about his Olympic journey, and to the late Joseph Campbell, for years of exercised talk about the virtues and perils of athletic competition. Thanks also to Bill Gallagher, Alexander and Jane Eliot, and Willis Barnstone for their help with translations and transliterations and for their general affection for all things Greek. I am also indebted to those kind souls who helped me with various aspects of my research, including David L. Miller, Will Evans, Susan Stafford, Gary Rhine, Rebecca Armstrong, Shriley J. Nicholson, Lawrence Beaton, Chris Donges, Margaret Wright, Mary Davis, and Tony Lawlor. My deep thanks, too, to Keith Thompson, for years of exuberant exchanges about the sporting life, and to Michael Murphy, for our sparkling discussions about the mystic side of sports. Thanks also to Tony and Janie at Caffe Sempione, in North Beach, for their caffeine courage and friendship.

Finally, there would be no book without the Penelope-like patience of my partner, Jo Beaton, and the boundless enthusiasm of our son and young Olympics fan, Jack.

Single is the race, single
Of men and of Gods;
From a single mother we both draw breath.
But a difference in power in everything
Keeps us apart . . .

— PINDAR

Man is a torch borne in the wind.

—RALPH WALDO EMERSON

He who is not courageous enough to take risks will accomplish nothing in life.

—MUHAMMAD ALI,
Olympic boxing champion

The Boxer, *bronze statue by*
Apollonius of Athens, 1st *century,* B.C.E.

INTRODUCTION

---※---

THE OLYMPIC SPIRIT
THE SECRET STRENGTH OF THE GREAT GAMES

As if resting from an epic competition, he had not moved for centuries. He was still lying on the sea floor when a scuba diver discovered him in an ancient wreck site in the turquoise waters of the Adriatic, just off the coast of Croatia, in 1997. By then, the fourth-century-B.C.E. bronze athlete had broken into several pieces and become so encrusted with wildly colored salt deposits that he looked more like a rusty cannon than an Olympic champion.

Since the Adriatic athlete was hauled out of the sea, underwater archaeologists have been chipping away at his corrosive coating, piecing together his body, and reassembling his story. Like slow-motion photography in reverse, the restoration process is gradually allowing us to see the long-lost bronze in all his former glory. The scientists tell us he was one of thousands of life-sized athlete sculptures, or *apoxoyomenoi*, created in honor of the victors at the Panhellenic Games and erected in their hometowns all over the ancient Greek world. Around the first century C.E., they say, he was being transported—probably to a

Roman palace or villa—when his ship sank and he tumbled down into "the blue museum," as fishermen across the Mediterranean describe the vast underwater "art gallery" of lost statues, pottery, and coins.

Shipwreck was an unexpected blessing for the Adriatic athlete. Most sculpture of the ancient world met a far worse fate. Nearly all the bronze statues were melted down for their metal, while the marble ones were crushed in limekilns to be used as mortar. He is one the few survivors, and the story of his odyssey and metamorphosis is worthy of Homer and Ovid. His luster has returned; the glint is back in his eyes. His expression is determined but calm, conveying his character's inner strength and outer beauty and recalling other fabled athlete statues, such as the graceful *Discus Thrower*, the winsome *Spartan Girl Runner*, the haunting *Charioteer*, and the brooding *Boxer*.

But there is another quality—a *force*—that deepens the mystery of these statues, especially in their connection to the Greek passion for athletic festivals, including the one the Greeks revered most of all, the Olympic Games. It is in fact the miraculous force that animates all great art as well as great athletes. Call it *spirit*, the divine spark, the breath of life—it is the transcendent element that lifts us up when we're down and out, the source of courage, and the soul of inspiration. Strangely, we're not quite sure where it comes from, where it goes when it's crushed, or how to revive it. We just know we need to be in touch with it, which is one reason we turn to art, drama, poetry, and sports, especially the Olympic Games, the most watched television event on earth. As the Games unfold every four years, we may be impressed by the skills of the world's greatest young athletes; but what *moves* us is what novelist and soccer fan Nick Hornsby calls "the thrilling flash of their spirit." That mysterious movement of spirit—from an athlete's *aspiration* for a great performance to our *inspiration* from witnessing it—is at the heart of the age-old fascination with all great games, which is what lies, in turn, at the center of this book.

The Olympic Odyssey chronicles the long history of the Olympic Games, from their origins in eighth-century-B.C.E. Greece through the twenty-two Olympiads held at sites across the globe since their revival, which, like Odysseus himself coming home, return to Greece for the 2004 Games. The focus of the book reflects my fascination with the interplay between the outer history of the Games—their facts and figures—and the inner history, which is revealed in their mythology, psychology, and poetry. Only in the latter can we find the deep roots of our ancient urge to play, to compete, and to excel; only there can we glimpse the birth of courage in an athlete, compassion in a coach, devotion in a fan.

I am haunted by the "flashes of spirit" that transcend ordinary athletic competition, especially during the sporting fantasia that unfolds at the Olympics. And I am bewitched by the impassioned efforts of well-known and unknown athletes alike, from around the world, to participate in peaceful competition. To me, these inspired efforts echo what nineteenth-century scholar E. Lowes Dickinson described in *The Greek View of Life* as the genius of ancient Greece philosophy—the uncanny ability to make oneself "at home in the world," even in an increasingly rootless world such as ours.

REVISITING
THE ANCIENT IDEAL

The Olympics have fired my imagination since I was a young boy, raised on the classics but saved by sports. Ours was a home familiar with Homer and homers, great books and great games, and the urge to fight for one's faith. I learned early on about the famous Greek ideal of strength and beauty—the harmony of a sound mind in a sound body—because my father insisted that I learn to balance balls with books. Meanwhile, my mother transferred me from a public to a parochial school so I could go to mass every morning and be infused with a sense of respect, if not awe and wonder, for the spiritual life.

"Thank goodness for the Phoenicians—or whoever it was—who invented books," my dad used to sigh as he picked up his favorite copy of Herodotus's *Histories* or Mark Twain's *Innocents Abroad*. "Faith moves mountains," my mother used to whisper when she felt she had to remind me why she had switched my schools.

As our family slowly disintegrated during my teens, I took refuge in the soul of the street—playing baseball and basketball and running track. I grew to love the way my skills and my spirit were tested. Sports saved me from a life of abstraction; it took me out of my head and out of church and thrust me right into my body.

From teachers and priests I may have learned about the great ideas of history, but from coaches and fellow athletes I learned the exciting fact that these ideas could be put into action on the field, on the court, and around the track. That's where I developed the fierce work habits, competitiveness, and determination that I have tapped into ever since. That's where I learned that along with the fire in the soul that the priests talked about, and the fire in the mind that my college professors advocated, there is an equally noble fire in the heart, in the body, that my coaches and my sports heroes taught me how to kindle—and rekindle again and again.

No wonder my ideal for the well-lived life has so closely paralleled the classical one—the passionate struggle for excellence in the pursuits of mind, body, and soul. And no wonder my admiration for this ancient Greek vision and inspiration to live an encyclopedic—literally, all-around—life has been tempered and frustrated in this day and age. For me, the joys of books, art, religion, and sports are inextricably connected. So it has been a source of utter exasperation that terrific cultural forces have kept them as far apart as possible. It's as if they were brawling boxers, pulled apart by the referees of academia, the clergy, and the various commissars of sports.

How can this have happened, since most educators give at least lip service to the ideal of the well-rounded life?

In *The Ultimate Athlete*, journalist and aikido master George Leonard identifies the source of the problem as philosophical: the infamous mind-body split, or more accurately, the mind-body-spirit split. This view, he writes, has been "a major error in Western thought, one that must never be repeated." Its implications are far reaching, from the classroom to the boardroom, from the studio to the stadium. "Athletes tend to become insensitive and authoritarian," he explains, and "intellectuals tend to become disembodied brains, unaware of the consequences of their thinking."

Rather than living in a culture that encourages athletes to meet with philosophers, artists with politicians, and soldiers with poets—as the ancient Greeks did for nearly twelve hundred years during the Festival of Zeus at ancient Olympia—we live in one where priests disdain the body, athletes dismiss thinkers, and everybody is suspicious of poets.

This is a surefire way to grow lopsided, like the shot-putter who only develops his throwing arm while his other arm withers, or the academic whose legs are too weak for a walk in the park. This divisive and destructive split can and must be repaired, insists Leonard, but it requires attention to making ourselves whole again. If we make this effort, he suggests tantalizingly, "Athletics can return to their rightful place of honor in the arts and humanities."

Such a change of view asks us to review the price we pay for the one-dimensional view of life, which produces the intense focus required for any form of success—yet with it the obsessiveness that threatens to ruin everything.

Going for the gold is a risky business.

GOLD AND GLORY

Founded at least twenty-eight hundred years ago in western Greece, abolished in the fourth century by the Roman tyrant Theodosius, and then revived with the loftiest of intentions in 1896, the Olympics have survived numerous ordeals to become what Pico Iyer calls "a model of our dreams of unity." He writes, in an essay that is a true "ode to the Olympic spirit," that Olympic Villages are microcosms of the global village and that in their most luminous moments they "pay homage to the very sense of 'world loyalty' that [philosopher Alfred North] Whitehead called the essence of religion." Perhaps that is why, for some, sports is merely a game, while for others it is a religion—and why it is often said, if you want to know the soul of a people, look at their collective behavior, watch how they *play,* pay attention to the way they *compete*.

The collective ecstasy expressed at the spectacular 2000 Sydney Games is ample evidence of the growing belief that when a city and a nation hosts the Olympics it is doing more than raising revenue, it is raising its profile on the world stage and baring its soul. Nearly two hundred nations and 10,000 athletes participated in those Games, while an estimated 3.7 billion people watched on television—the largest audience in history—all in the hopes of catching a fleeting glimpse of gold and glory.

The hunger for glory is as old as hunger itself. Ample evidence for it is found in hunting and war lore, as well as in epic literature, such as *Beowulf,* whose hero was "the keenest to win fame," or the *Iliad,* in which Achilles surrenders the promise of immortality for the glory granted only to valiant warriors. The deeply embedded impulse to chase down glory can spur warriors, athletes, and poets alike to do their best—even surpass their own limits—a glorious accomplishment in its own way. The great Greek poet Pindar, composer of odes to Olympic victors, suggests that the glory of the Games was that they allowed one man to be "separated out . . . distinguished by excellence." His only tangible reward for victory was a laurel wreath, but the intangible rewards, referred to as *kleos,* "the renown or fame that rewards hard-earned success," were infinite.

And what about all the talk of *gold,* the "gold rush," as sports writers call the push for the ultimate medal in all of sports? What is it about gold that motivated *Time* magazine's art designers to give the brilliant sprinter Marion Jones a coat of gold paint when they put her on the cover the week before the Sydney 2000 Games? Why will young athletes risk everything for the honor of wearing an Olympic gold medal?

The most precious of metals, gold symbolizes what is highest and purest. Thus gold carries spiritual meaning in many religious traditions. Gold's rarity and beauty have always evoked the irrepressible desire to possess it, often at any cost. The shadow side of gold is greed and corruptibility, which leads to "gold *fever.*" From King Midas's fatal wish that everything he touched be turned to gold to the California '49ers' mad rush for riches to medal-obsessed Olympic athletes, the lust for the immortal metal has always made good people do strange things. In the pressure cooker of competition, an athlete or coach can either *excel,* which is what the great ones do, or go *berserk,* as the Nordic bards called the frenzy of warriors in battle. The former is the stuff of legend; the latter results in cheating, doping, cruelty, and the corporate avarice that breeds bribery, corruption, and commercialism.

The pressure to win at all costs—whether in sports, art, religion, business, or the military—pervades modern life, but the pressure is hardly new. In the estimation of many Olympic historians, it was the perils of professionalism accompanying the secularization of the ancient Olympic Games, from about the fifth-century B.C.E. onward, that led to their long, slow decline. To read of the temptations that bedeviled athletes and taunted trainers in ancient times is to be reminded of how little human character has changed. The main difference is one of scale. The choices are the same: to play fair or take unfair advantage, to be a good sport or be mean-spirited, to do your best or slack off, to feel pride at having participated or bitterness for not having won.

One of this book's main themes is that we, as athletes, coaches, parents, and spectators, can choose how much influence gold and glory have over us—whether we will be blinded by the light or able to see better because our aim was higher. It all depends on where—and upon whom—we focus our attention. We can worship only winners, overwhelm ourselves with statistics, and obsess about which country is accumulating the most medals. Or we can watch for what the ancient Greek poets called "the infinite moment," the moment of truth, when courage, desire, and pride in the lone athlete or the bound-together team emerges—or doesn't.

This do-or-die moment is the very dramatization of life's struggle. It is the heart of art, literature, and athletics, and it's a beautiful thing when enacted with passion and grace. Our hunger for this drama is borne out in a poll taken by NBC Sports chairman Dick Ebersol. He commented, "About 80 percent of our viewers want to see the athletes *struggle* . . . They want to see their survival against amazing odds, and then their subsequent moment of victory or sadly, often times, their agonizing moment of defeat."

The polls bear out the universal fascination with stories of how human beings overcome ordeals. We may be impressed with natural talent, but we admire underdogs, scrappers, those who defy the odds and never quit, those who "make the impossible seem possible"—as a fellow bicyclist described Lance Armstrong after the Sydney Games. These are the Olympians who transcend the Games, like the one-legged gymnast George Eyser, who won five medals at the turn of the century; Marla Runyan, the legally blind 1,500-meter runner who competed in the 2000 Games by pacing herself alongside rivals, who appeared to her as "streaks of light"; and sprinter Gail Devers, who contracted Graves' disease and nearly had her feet amputated but went on to win three gold medals at the 1988 Games. Their fabled stories can kindle a spark of inspiration that may inexplicably help us later get through our own dark nights of the soul.

Their stories also shed new light on the reputed epigraph to the American Dream, supposedly uttered by legendary American football coach Vince Lombardi: "Winning isn't everything, it's the only thing." However, Lombardi spent the last several years of his life claiming what he *really* said was, "Winning isn't everything—but making the *effort* to win is." The cultural forces that twisted his original words are constantly at work, transmogrifying our desire to do our best, or to witness other's efforts to do so, into settling for nothing other than winning, nothing less than "the killer instinct."

The NBC Sports report confirms our longing for more than statistics and star power; it vindicates our desire for the transcendent dimension of sports, the innate drama of one individual or one team struggling to do their best. We already know what it takes to get by in everyday life. What is infinitely harder is to know what it takes to get through the ordeals of extraordinary life, which is why we are held fast to great drama—at the theater, in the church, and in the stadium alike. We long to witness not just the talent that is shown off but the spirit that rises to the occasion, the courage that responds in a moment of truth. Our fascination with the revelation of fate, whether in a novel, a movie, or an Olympic competition, is boundless. As the Polish poet Adam Zagajewski has written, we long "to experience astonishment and to stop still in that astonishment for a long moment or two."

William J. Baker writes in *Sports in the Western World:* "Human beings cannot live by bread alone. They dream and they strive. Not merely for warmth do they take fire from the altar of the gods; curiosity is their glory and their pain. They climb mountains, cross uncharted seas, and explore outer space for reasons other than material benefit. They thrive on challenges. Seekers of laurels, they especially measure themselves in competition with fellow humans. Where there is no contest, they create one. From deep within, and from millennia past, comes the impulse for athletic competition."

In *The Heart of a Champion*, esteemed sports writer Frank Deford comments, "Ultimately, as frivolous as our games may seem to be, courage in sports does matter a great deal. Most forms of courage aren't especially visible. Most courage, in fact, is quiet . . . But still we need to know of courage, to see it on display, so that by visible example we may be emboldened to take a risk ourselves someday . . . that is, to see courage on the hoof."

To witness courage on display requires a test, preferably a contest, a competition, as the ancient Greeks knew well. David C. Young writes in *The Modern Olympics* that the ancient athletic contest represented "the general Greek struggle to rise above man's essentially ephemeral, abject condition and do what a man cannot ordinarily do . . . Only performance and achievement counted."

If there was a secret to the Greeks' genius for the well-lived life, it had to do with this fiery conviction that the ordinary citizen could become extraordinary if he was encouraged to compete, and could be praised into immortality if he excelled. Victory was considered sweet at any of the hundreds of ancient Greek athletic festivals, but sweetest of all at Olympia, because the Games were dedicated to Zeus and considered to have the most integrity.

The modern Olympics were inaugurated in 1896 with lofty intentions to continue that sacred legacy. But the modern Games are "struggling to maintain their integrity," write Robert K. Barney and the other authors of the exposé *Selling the Five Rings*. "On the one hand, the Olympic Movement now has the resources to carry forward the spiritual ideals for which it has always stood. On the other hand, the very sources of wealth that permit the extension of its ideals to the world threaten to undermine the purity and nobility of its crusade."

There are probing questions at the heart of *The Olympic Odyssey*. What have the ancient Greeks and the revivers of the Games passed down to us and what do we wish to pass on to the next generation? What is the transcendent element that uplifts athlete, coach, and fan alike? Is it enthusiasm—literally being "filled with the gods"—or is it the perennial dream of brotherhood, the ancient dream of peace? Will we be content to treat the Games as merely one more source of entertainment, or will we look to them as exhilarating stages on which great dramas of the human spirit are acted out? What price are we paying for glamorizing our athletes and hyping the Games as we do? What is it about the Olympic torch that moves us so?

PASSING THE TORCH

In modern times we believe fire is merely a physical phenomenon, a combustion of molecules that results in light, flame, and heat. But numerous myths around the world reveal a human reverence for fire, a widespread belief that fire is sacred, a gift from nature that once belonged to the gods and that they guarded with tenacity. The Aztecs dispatched ultra–long distance runners, trained to cover more than a hundred miles a day, with ceremonial torches lit from their sacred fires to be shared with distant villages and occasionally rekindled in the main temple. The Papago Indian leaders were named "Keepers of the Fire," and each one had his own personal messenger, called his "Leg." The Leg's task was to tend the sacred fire and run messages of war *and* peace, as in challenges of peaceful athletic competition, to other tribes. The ancient Greeks believed Zeus intentionally made life difficult for human beings when "he hid fire," in the words of Hesiod. This ruse provoked Prometheus into stealing it right back and presenting it to human beings, a cosmic gift for which he paid a dire price.

The classical scholar Philostratus echoes this primal fascination with fire in his picaresque story of the original *stade*, or footrace, at Olympia being a race to the Altar of Zeus for the honor of lighting the sacrificial fire with the victor's torch. Modern scholars M. L. Finley and H. W. Pleket write that local torch races were common in antiquity, with teams of runners "wearing diadems, carrying their lighted torches in metal holders through the streets 'from altar to altar.'"

The torch relay was not part of the ancient Games but was choreographed by German officials to add glamour and ancient cachet to the opening ceremonies at the 1936 Berlin Games. It has since become one of the modern Games' most authentically heart-moving rituals. The ceremonial act of passing the sacred torch symbolizes the ideal of international brotherhood and is meant to remind us of the unity of nations. Every four years the torch is ignited by the sun's rays at the altar in the temple of

Hera, in ancient Olympia, and carried by relay to the current Olympic site. Thousands of runners pass the torch, hand to hand, from city to city, country to country, while millions of people line the roads and highways of the world, cheering for the runner and the torch.

Symbolic of enlightenment, purification, fertility, heat, and light, the torch is a powerful image. But the simple *transfer* of the torch as it is handed from one runner to the next moves us in our very souls. I recall standing on the Golden Gate Bridge in the cold fog one early morning in 1984, along with thousands of others. We were waiting alongside a shivering teenage girl in a T-shirt and shorts until an elderly man in a gray sweatshirt came jogging down the highway from the Marin hills. He held the Olympic torch high and with a sense of triumph passed it to her so she could take it across the bridge.

Slowly, the torch made its way down the coast to Los Angeles for the Games. When the torch finally arrived at the entrance to the Colosseum, it was ceremoniously handed off to Jesse Owens's granddaughter, Gina, who ran a lap around the track to thunderous applause. The din grew louder when she relayed the torch one last time to Rafer Johnson, winner of the 1956 decathlon in Melbourne, who climbed the steep steps of the stadium to light the Olympic ring of fire, which blazed throughout the Games.

Eight years later, the world watched on television as the once formidable boxing champion, Muhammad Ali, arguably the most beloved athlete of our time, struggled to light the cauldron at the 1992 Barcelona Games because of the tremors of Parkinson's disease. At the 2000 Sydney Games, the ancient Olympic dream of reconciliation was revived when Cathy Freeman, outstanding Australian Aborigine sprinter, was the chosen one to ignite the Olympic flame.

© IOC/Olympic Museum Collections

Muhammad Ali, the 1960 Olympic heavyweight
boxing gold-medal winner, returned in 1992
to light the cauldron at Barcelona.

What is it in these gestures that moves us so deeply? Does it remind us that life itself is a race against time, that we have only so much time to pass along whatever we have learned about life to the next generation? "On what wings dare he aspire?" the mystic poet Blake asks. "What the hand dare seize the fire?"

Native American elders say that we must keep the gift of life *moving*. This is soulful advice for everyday life. In regards to the exalted life of the Olympics, it provokes us to ask: What is the gift of the Games that we—athletes, coaches, parents, spectators, and media alike—wish to pass along?

These questions were on Jesse Owens's mind in the months and years after his courageous performance at the Berlin Games, where he stunned the Nazi leaders by winning four gold medals. As the grandson of slaves and the son of a sharecropper, Owens knew the symbolic importance of his achievement for black people in America. But he also knew that far more happened to him in Berlin than setting world records and being crowned with laurel. He writes in his autobiography that he had gone all the way to Europe hoping to find the true meaning of the Olympics, only to discover that "Life—the inner life—is the true Olympics." From his ordeals with the Nazis and from the friendship he formed with his main rival, German long jumper Luz Long, he learned that "Spiritual strength is more important than physical strength."

When Owens returned to America, he passed the torch of his hard-earned wisdom as flawlessly as he passed the baton in the world-record-setting relays. "I have devoted the majority of my hours since," he writes, "attempting to inspire others to feel what I feel, know what I now know."

For Owens and many other Olympic athletes, the gold is *inward*, the reward is more invisible than visible, and the gift is so powerful that it must be kept alive by involving athletes and coaches in their communities long after the torch is extinguished at the end of each Olympiad. If it is true, as Emerson said, that, "Man is a torch borne in the wind," then when we see the Olympic torch rekindled we know the holy fire is alive and well in the human race.

Ruins of the gymnasium at ancient Olympia, with Mount Kronos in the distance.

THE JOURNEY

On the surface, the Games are only games, a rhapsody on the theme of athletic competition, even if at the most elite level. Below the surface, however, the tectonic plates of the mythic imagination are at work, revealing the numinous feeling that accompanies the Games. To understand the deeper working of the Games, we must take a journey into myth, the root story, the story of how things came to be, because it is myth that returns us to the sacred origins of everything—including sports—to know their deeper nature, their *secret strength*. The beginning of human play and contests is also the little-explored zone where competition meets mythology and culture. Out of the myriad themes that could emerge from this rich realm, I have chosen six to comprise the chapters of this book.

These themes include the mythic origins of the Olympics, the sacred connection between gods and games, the ritual significance of the sacred festival, the revival of the Games, the pursuit of excellence, and the inspired role of the philosopher-coach. An epilogue lists suggestions for rekindling the spirit and restoring the joy of the Games for athletes and fans alike. Together, the discussions in these chapters are meant to complement the current realities of the Olympic Games, rife with ferocious economic and nationalistic competition, with the transcendent possibilities, those that allow us to "rise above ourselves," that the Games have held out since their origins.

As we embark upon our Olympic odyssey, it is important to recall historian Will Durant's qualifier concerning the Greek gift to civilization: "We know its defects—its insane and pitiless wars, its stagnant slavery, its subjection of women, its lack of moral restraint, its corrupt individualism, its tragic failure to unite liberty with order and peace. But those who cherish freedom, reason, and beauty will not linger over these blemishes . . . They will think of Greece as the bright morning of that Western civilization which, with all its kindred faults, is our nourishment and our life."

Similarly, dwelling too long on the defects of sports is like focusing on the corrosion masking the beauty of the recovered athlete statues, or being too anesthetized by the modern Games' excesses to access the vision of courage underneath them. Other books have focused on the Games' lamentable flaws, such as doping and commodification. Still others recount the minutiae of statistics and record-breaking feats. What concerns this book is the spirit that Olympic athletes carry within themselves and that the world responds to as if to a holy fire.

"Spirit is not always visible in sports," writes Michael Novak in *The Joy of Sports*, "it is not always actualized; [it] is often dormant. But at any moment it may flash through."

Like all true odysseys, this book is a meandering journey in search of the spirit that has always animated the great games in our lives. Along the way, we will review what it really means to *win*, an old English word whose roots reach down to *strife* and *conflict*, but also to *joy* and *delight*. As many commentators have said, the great test of the contest is whether the athlete, the player, or the coach exhibit joy during the competition. In a mysterious way, which we will explore throughout this book, there is no true success, no victory, no winning, if there is no joy. As the long history of the Olympics shows, it is just as possible to win and still lose as it is to lose and still win. But we don't know that for sure unless we know the soul-strengthening moments of courage and overcoming terrific odds to excel. As the baseball wag Yogi Berra said, "There are deep depths here."

"We don't just tell stories," said Sidney Mills, a Lakota Sioux man, to his young son, Billy, in the early 1950s. "We tell stories to teach a lesson. Anything you can learn life lessons from is sacred."

The Olympic spirit of the Games is a beautiful thing, as Billy Mills revealed years later, at the 1964 Tokyo Games, in a fabled performance that has become part of the sacred lore of his people. But it must be rekindled, nurtured, and tended, like the sacred fire as it travels along the relay or the fire of desire spotted by the alert coach. This book celebrates the holy fire within the flame of competition; it acknowledges the passing of the torch of hope that the Games' display of beauty, strength, and excellence can enhance the human spirit.

Like all great dramas of the human condition, the Games are a mirror held up to us, asking, as poet Mary Oliver does:

> Listen, are you breathing just a little,
> and calling it a life?

If only a little, why not *more?* Why are you not breathing hard and fast, as if in the most exhilarating race, striving to do your best, to reach for the laurels, the life of excellence? Is that not what every Olympiad asks of us—to reflect on the game of life within the Game? This is the secret strength of the Games. As Olympic filmographer Bud Greenspan has said so memorably in *The Hundred Greatest Moments in Olympic History*, the noble challenge is for athletes to "enter the arena, make our attempt, and pursue excellence. And because of their effort, all of us go back to our homes the better for it."

What sets our hearts on fire is worth passing on.

OLYMPIA

SACRED PLAYGROUND OF GODS AND HEROES

Let everyone exercise his own art.
—ARISTOPHANES

This scale model shows how the ancient Greeks' beloved sanctuary would have appeared in 100 B.C.E. By the Middle Ages, decimated by floods and earthquakes, it was buried under thirteen feet of silt. The English explorer Richard Chandler discovered it in 1766 only by chance when he came upon the ruins of the Temple of Zeus.

A *Gymnasium:* Constructed in the 2nd century B.C.E., the gymnasium was used for training runners and throwers. Its four colonnades provided shelter during bad weather, and discus and javelin throwing took place in the courtyard.

B *Palaistra:* The exercise ground for wrestlers and jumpers, this 3rd century B.C.E. structure of colonnades around a courtyard included nineteen rooms for oiling, powdering, bathing, and general training.

C *Temple of Hera:* Dating from c. 600 B.C.E., the goddess's temple was the first built at Olympia, before the immigrant Elians supplanted goddess worship with their warrior god, Zeus. The temple housed paintings of the victors of the women's events, called the Games of Hera.

D *Treasuries:* At the foot of Mount Kronus, named for Zeus's father, stood eleven small, temple-like buildings, each built by a Greek colony to house their valuables and proclaim their prestige.

E *Stadium:* With a track of clay covered with sand, the 4th century B.C.E. stadium was 105 feet wide and 630 feet long—the distance we are told that Herakles, mythical founder of the Games, ran in one breath. Its embankments could hold 45,000 spectators.

F *Swimming Pool:* Unique in ancient Greece, the 5th century B.C.E. open-air pool was about 79 feet long by 52 feet wide and 5 feet deep—just a little smaller than a public pool today.

G *Leonidaion:* Named after Leonidas of Naxos, its 4th century B.C.E. funder, this building was a hotel for officials and VIPs.

H *Sacred Olive Tree:* Planted by Herakles (according to Pindar), the sacred tree provided branches for the victors' crowns.

I *Temple of Zeus:* Supported by thirty-four columns, this remarkable structure, completed in 456 B.C.E., took ten years to build. Inside it stood a marble figure of Zeus almost forty-three feet high and a golden statue of Nike, Goddess of Victory. Adorning its pediments were relief sculptures depicting the twelve labors of Herakles.

J *Southern colonnade:* From this graceful, 4th century B.C.E. structure, the Games' judges may have staged ceremonies to welcome the horse-drawn chariots entering the Hippodrome.

K *Hippodrome:* The *hippodrome* (horse track) provided a lap just under ¾ of a mile long for a spread of chariots forty feet wide. Atop the finishing post were bronze figures depicting the fabled origin of equestrian events: Hippodamia crowning Pelops after he outraced her father, King of Pisa.

THE
MYTHIC ORIGINS

---❋---

THE SPIRIT OF PLACE AND
THE SOUL OF SPORTS

*With regard to the Olympic games,
the Elean antiquaries say that Kronos
first reigned in Heaven, and that a temple
was made for him by the men of that age,
who were named the Golden Race...*

—Pausanius, second century C.E.

The most important thing in the Olympic Games is not to win but to take part; the important thing in life is not the triumph but the struggle.

— BARON PIERRE DE COUBERTIN,
founder of the modern Olympic movement

———— ✳ ————

Never a city, always a sanctuary, Olympia has been regarded as a sacred site for untold thousands of years. The spirit is strong there, the sense of presence undeniable. The roots of reverence run deep. If Delphi was the *omphalos*, the mythic navel, of the ancient Greek world, then Olympia was its mythic heart.

Olympia lies a few miles from the sea in the northern Peloponnese, in a serene valley flanked by mountains at the point where the Alpheios River meets the Kladeos. Situated thirty miles from the nearest major city, Elis, which ruled over the sanctuary through its glory days, Olympia is worlds apart from the rocky reality of other Greek sites. Warm, fertile, and scented by wildflowers, the voluptuous valley was beloved by the ancient Greeks. Their poets wrote that its tranquility inspired the idea of reconciliation among the constantly warring city-states whose citizens visited the sanctuary. The Greek word for the area—*Arcadia*—has come down to us virtually unchanged as the name of a distant paradise, a region of simple pleasures and untroubled people. As Roberto Calasso writes, "Olympia was the home of happiness to the ancient Greeks, who knew unhappiness better than any other people." This mythic memory is a key to understanding the grip the Olympics have had on the world's imagination for the past twenty-eight hundred years.

The sacred nature of Olympia was recognized by its earliest settlers and pilgrims, who believed the land belonged to the gods and goddesses. They sought out the oracle who dwelled in a rock cleft high on the Hill of Kronus; made sacrifices at the altars of the goddess Ge, or Gaia; conducted rituals in honor of Themis, goddess of justice; and held fertility festivals in honor of the earth mother, Ilithyia, and her divine child, Sosipolis.

According to ancient Greek history, Olympia was the site of various funeral games, military exercises, or local religious events as early as the thirteenth century B.C.E. Then a hundred years later, in the twelfth century B.C.E., waves of tribes—Achaeans, Dorians, and Elians—descended from the north and inundated the valley. These early Greek immigrants muscled their way into the goddesses' ancient sanctuary along the banks of the Alpheus and replaced them with their agrarian warrior god, Zeus. This transfer of power was symbolically portrayed in Olympia's founding myth when Zeus boldly claimed ownership of the sacred grove with a single javelinlike toss of his thunderbolt from his palace on Mount Olympus, as if signifying the spirit of the human ritual play that would follow. The scorched bit of earth where his bolt struck was marked by the ashen altar where Zeus was later worshipped, and the sacred ground in front of the altar became the staging area for the first athletic contests.

Legend has it that these rudimentary competitions were first organized into distinct Games in the twelfth century B.C.E. by their leader, King Oxylus. For the next few centuries, the Elians paid tribute to Zeus in the form of sacrifices, prayers, and races held in the sacred precinct. Then, for reasons lost to the ravages of time, the Games were abandoned. Ancient chronicles tell us that by the eighth century B.C.E. the Greeks had forgotten the Games ever existed—and were in dire misery because of it. They needed divine inspiration to remind them about the healing power of ritual play and peaceful competition. When the Games resumed in 776 B.C.E., they were considered sacred contests. Their revival so impressed the Greeks that they declared that date the very beginning of their history, and it is when the Greek calendar officially starts. From then on, the whole society measured time, not in political terms, as we might refer to "the Kennedy era," but in terms of their most revered champion sprinters—as in, "Back in the time of Ageus of Argos, victor in the 113th Olympiad . . ."

THE FIRST REVIVAL

But how did it all begin? asks Italian classical scholar Roberto Calasso in *The Marriage of Cadmus and Harmony*, his spellbinding book on Greek mythology. As he suggests by incantatorily posing this question again and again, if you want to know the many-layered meanings of the sacred stories that describe our bittersweet relationship with the gods, you must seek out the origins of everything that matters to the soul.

But how did it all begin? This is the question that launched a thousand myths. The ship of sacred story sets sail every time a human being asks how things came to be. Our ancient and modern myths are deep narratives that provide us with the *inner meaning* of outer events, root stories that allow us to trace things down to their depths.

Given the power and influence of myth, it is helpful for anyone who seriously questions the relevance of the ancient or modern Olympics to seek their mythic origins. Unless we distinguish the nature of those origins and understand how they still influence us today, David C. Young writes, "We will never perceive how legitimate it is to call our modern Games 'Olympic Games.'"

The mythic origins of Olympia's sacred games—symbolically the dawn of organized athletic activity for the entire Western world—is a tale with a thousand faces. Myths are protean—shape-shifting and ever-changing—because the truth of our interior life is inexhaustible. Thus, the ancients said, there is no one true reading of a myth. All versions are true because all are needed to complete the original story. For this reason, all of the Olympic origin stories bear repeating at the beginning of every modern version of the Games.

Some say the polyfabulous—many-storied—Games began when Zeus wrestled with his father, Kronus, the Titan god of time, on the hilltop overlooking the sacred grove at Olympia. This wrestling match would become symbolic of the titanic struggle with time itself, as well as the inborn competition between fathers and sons.

By the fifth century B.C.E., the honor of founding the Games had been passed to Herakles. One variation of the story tells of his arrival from Mount Ida on Crete, olive branch in hand, with his four brothers, who slept on olive branches with him and ran against him in a footrace. Herakles himself measured the distance they would run by pacing six hundred steps, or two hundred meters, which was called a *stadia,* the origins of our word *stadium.* The great hero is also credited with declaring that the Games be held every fifth year (by the ancient Greek calendar; four by our modern calendar) in honor of himself and his four brothers. The memory of these heroic gestures instilled in the ancient Greeks the ideal of brotherhood being sustained even in the heat of competition. The recognition of teammates and opponents alike as brothers or sisters remains one of the goals of modern sports.

Male figures running, Greek redware pottery, circa 2nd century.
Note the high-arm action denoting sprinters.

Pindar, visiting Olympia in the first century, heard another version of the Herakles founding myth. The Games were established, he was told, after Herakles' victory over Augeas, when the hero ingeniously diverted a local river to clean the noxious stables. In William H. Race's translation, Pindar's Eleventh Olympian Ode reads:

> Thereupon, Zeus' valiant son gathered the entire army
> And all the booty of Pisa,
> And measured out a sacred precinct for his father
> Most mighty. He fenced in the Altis and set it apart
> In the open, and he made the surrounding plain

A resting place for banqueting . . .
    and at that founding ceremony
The fates stood near at hand,
As did the sole assayer
Of genuine truth, Time . . .
He then founded
The quadrennial festival with the first Olympiad
And its victories.

Herakles' godlike feats of strength, courage, and selflessness of spirit became the model for athletes all over the ancient Greek world. Yet he embodied the very spirit of the ancient Greeks for reasons beyond his legendary power: he was loved by the gods— so much so that they allowed him to become one himself.

Another origin myth attributes the Games' founding to Pelops. One of the great authorities on the Olympics, E. Norman Gardiner, writes, "Pelops was certainly the chief local hero of Olympia. There he had a shrine and was worshipped as a hero. In late times it was supposed that the [Olympic] festival originated in the funeral games held at his tomb."

The grisly story of Pelops, son of Tantalus, torn asunder by his father and brought back to life by the pitying gods, is suffused with symbolism. After the gods revived him they gave him a golden chariot, which he used to drive across the Aegean in search of a wife. He took up the challenge for the hand of a beautiful princess, Hippodameia, daughter of Oenomaus, king of Pisa, near Elis. All he had to do was compete in a do-or-die chariot race against her father. If he lost, he would be slain by the king. Twelve other suitors had died for lack of speed and cunning. Pelops swore he would not be the thirteenth. He bribed Myrtilus, the king's master charioteer, to replace the iron thole pins in the king's chariot with wax pins, and near the end of the race the king was thrown to his death. Pelops won the princess and the kingdom. In thanksgiving, it was said, Pelops founded the Games, highlighted by chariot races that were a ritual reenactment of his own triumph over an otherwise cruel fate.

However, as the story reminds us, Pelops paid a price for his chicanery. Soon after the chariot race he silenced the king's charioteer by hurling him over a nearby cliff, but not before Myrtilus cursed Pelops and all his descendants, which included his doomed sons, Atreus and Thyestes.

Compressed into this grim but poignant story are threads relevant to our own athletic competition—the reward that often comes out of a life of sacrifice, the cosmic marriage of beauty and strength, the metaphor of life as a race against death, the dire price that is paid for attempting to win at all costs.

Each variation on the origins of the ancient Olympic Games so far related rings out with rich insight, but perhaps the most compelling of all is the legend from the Greek Dark Ages, around the ninth century B.C.E., concerning King Iphitus of Elis, a descendant of King Oxylus.

According to the chronicles, King Iphitus grieved deeply. His land had been laid to waste by endless war and plague. As was the custom of the time for peasants and kings alike, he sought advice from the oracle of Delphi. Upon his arrival at the temple of Apollo, the good king told the priestess he longed to know a way to end the warfare and heal the disease that ravaged his land.

As Judith Swaddling of the British Museum writes, "The priestess advised that he should restore the Olympic Games and declare a truce for their duration." For King Iphitus, the priestess's pithy reply was clear enough, but he wondered about the deeper implications of her holy counsel. Tradition tells us that Iphitus nevertheless eventually signed a treaty with Lycourgos, king of Sparta, and Cleisthenes, king of Pisa, to ensure no fighting for a month before and after the festival so pilgrims, spectators, athletes, and trainers could travel safely and coexist peacefully at Olympia. The treaty was inscribed on a discus and kept in the Herarion, the temple to Hera, at Olympia.

Regardless of whether the oracle's role in the story is history or fiction, Swaddling adds, the astonishing longevity of the Games speaks to the truce's vitality. "The Olympic Truce was a major instrument in the unification of the Greek states and colonies."

For historians and literary scholars, the legend of the king and the oracle is evidence that organized games were staged at Olympia at least a century before 776 B.C.E., the Games' official beginning. Historically, the treaty helped forge the national and spiritual unity of the Greek nation, but mythically its message of peaceful reconciliation extended across centuries to influence the later revival of the Games, in Athens in 1896—as well as to provide hope for fans of the modern Games.

The legend of King Iphitus reveals another aspect of athletics' spiritual dimension. The king's pilgrimage to the oracle and her response reveal that sacred games—athletic competition with a deeper purpose—are *divinely inspired* as a way to help human beings sublimate their most violent instincts. The legend says that there was a time when we played sacred games and that they helped make us peaceful. The world is at war, it says,

This rare photograph of an "International Tug of War" contest—won by the Milwaukee AC team—at the 1904 St. Louis Olympics is emblematic of the ancient Greek dream of transforming the urge to violence through playful competition.

because we have forgotten how to compete in the game of life. We must remember how to participate in competitions not for ourselves alone but for the honor of the gods, our families, or our homelands.

In his guidebook to the Olympic ruins, Greek archaeologist Manolis Andronicos comments on the Games' subliminal message: "The supreme significance of the Games demanded that all be present in peaceful assembly in the sacred grove." Both athletes and spectators, he says, couldn't help but notice that friends and foes alike were mingling peacefully without fear of violence. Often, men who had fought one another in battle were now fighting in peace. The Games were a golden opportunity for one and all to contemplate the dream of Greek unity.

No one pretended that the Games would permanently replace war. The Greeks loved battle too much—as symbolized by the marriage of Aphrodite and Ares, the gods of love and war—to dispense with it permanently. But as their mythic marriage shows, the fusion of the two—loving combat—can bring Harmony (the name of their love child) into the world.

Mythically and psychologically, this is what the ancient Games provided—an ideal, a model, along the lines of the inspired dramas of Euripides, the poems of Pindar, and the speeches of Pericles—a transcendent vision of our better selves. The loss of this uplifting vision, the legend suggests, leads to disintegration of the land and despair, as embodied by the sorrowful king.

The Olympic Games evolved into the time and place where Greeks of all city-states came together for religious ceremonies, artistic and athletic competition, and opportunities for reconciliation. Historian Will Durant writes in *The Life of Greece*, "Religion failed to unify Greece, athletics—periodically—succeeded . . . Under the rubric of athletics we find the real religion of the Greeks—the worship of health, beauty, and strength."

Third-century Greek poet Articlorus illuminated the link between religion and sport when he wrote: "Learn the rhythm that binds all men." If sport is the rhythm of movement, religion is the belief system that *binds us* together (from *re-liger*). The religion of sport is the love of games, which binds us together as a city, a nation, or ideally, in our own time, the entire human community.

In ancient Greece, inspired by tales of wondrous events, every fourth year pilgrims, athletes, trainers, and spectators made the meandering journey to Olympia from every corner of the known world. The five-day long Olympiad, the Festival of Zeus, combined elaborate religious ceremonies with art and athletics in a fusion of festivities scarcely imaginable today.

For nearly twelve hundred years—293 Olympiads—the pilgrimages and contests continued virtually without interruption. After the Roman occupation of Greece, in 142 B.C.E., however, the Games steadily deteriorated. Finally, in 393 C.E. the crazed Roman emperor Theodosius ordered the destruction of all pagan temples throughout the empire, including those at Olympia, and banned the Games. A Christian basilica was constructed over Phidias's workshop, where he had built the statue of Zeus and where, it is rumored, the Venus de Milo was carved. The sanctuary became a marble quarry for distant churches and villas. Earthquakes and floods slowly buried the entire site thirty feet deep in silt.

The last documented champion, his triumph recorded in 369 C.E., was Prince Barasdates, a boxer from Armenia.

THE SECOND REVIVAL: ATHENS, 1896

For the next fifteen hundred years, the fabled Greek ideal of "a healthy mind in a healthy body" faded, like frescoes exposed to light and air. Olympia and her Games were entombed but not forgotten; the stories of valor and strength submerged but not lost, the sacred roots of modern sports smothered with the earth but alive. The Olympic idea of a *way of life* based on the ideal *kalou k'agathou*—beauty, health, and virtue—awaited its second revival. In Roman times the purpose of sport was to provide, in Juvenal's famous phrase, "blood and the games of the circus" but also to maintain the high military standards demanded by the emperors. The organized games held in Roman amphitheaters, however, likewise declined, yielding to what John Arlott, in *Pageantry of Sport,* calls "the localized, sometimes religiously inspired, but largely spontaneous play of the Middle Ages and the extravagancies of the Regency."

Over the centuries, the desire to play games for sheer amusement continued unabated because, as Arlott writes, "the spirit is, ultimately, unquenchable." Despite draconian local laws against playing seemingly harmless games, the ordinary Englishman persisted in playing "football, cards, quoits, bowls, boxing, and cock-fighting" and on Sundays and holy days perhaps indulging in singing and dancing. For large-scale organized games to resume, more leisure time was required, along with a change in the patronage of sport and a vision of sport as something beyond amusement and diversion. These conditions were not available until the early nineteenth century.

The modern origin myth for the revival of the Games usually redounds upon Baron Pierre de Coubertin, a patriotic Frenchman associated with the Sorbonne in the early 1890s. In the preface to the Album of the Olympic Games of 1896, Coubertin writes, "It is generally difficult to understand why and how an idea is conceived and becomes reality, emerging from the string of other ideas waiting to be realized . . . This is not the case, however, with the Olympic Games . . . The idea for the revival of the Games was not an idle fancy; it was the logical outcome of a grand movement." Later, he would say he had been inspired by the tragedies of the Prussian War to ensure that the future would be brighter, and he believed peace and a civilized world were contingent upon the health and vitality of the world's youth, upon what he called a new "religion of sport."

Many at the time derided Coubertin for his nostalgic views—meaning *nostalgia* in the pejorative sense of a sentimental longing for the past, rather than its original reference to a deep longing for home as found in Homer's *Odyssey*, the story of the hero's return to Ithaca. As Coubertin presented it, the modern Olympic movement was a return to an original vision of athletic competition as a fusion of beauty and health, and it echoed too another ancient Greek sensibility, the display of brotherhood and peaceful competition.

The true tale of the rebirth, however, is far more colorful and international. The reigning expert on the history of the modern Games is the classicist David C. Young. He discovered, after years of painstaking sleuthing in England, Germany, and Greece, that the real origins of the "Great Revival" go back decades before the now-legendary Games in Athens in 1896. His research reveals that Coubertin's concoction of a "boyhood vision" of resurrecting the noble Greek Games was pure myth-making, in the lesser meaning of the word. A cache of copious correspondence between Coubertin and early revivalists in England and Greece proves that the baron knew of two nascent attempts to revive the Olympics long before he convened the famous Sorbonne Congress in Paris in 1892.

The bulk of Young's argument is based on communications between Coubertin and William Penny Brookes, organizer of the earliest attempts at revival—the Much Wenlock Games in England, founded in 1850 and held again on a national level in London in 1866. Young also brings to light letters between Coubertin and a young Greek journalist and poet named Panagiotis Soutsos, whose vision of a revival including athletic festivals and the arts helped inspire the so-called Zappian Games in Athens in 1859.

The Greek historian Dimitra Pikramenou-Varfi traces the very first stirrings of the Greek cultural rebirth even earlier, to the early nineteenth century in the Ionian islands, where the French imperial rulers announced the Prix Olympiques as an integral part of their new cultural policy. The awards were for artistic competitions rather than athletic contests, but the seed of pride in Greece's ancient glory had been planted. Not long after, in the 1830s, Soutsos had his vision. In *The Modern Olympics* Young writes:

> It began as sheer poetry . . . Soutsos seemed to have stumbled on an Olympic rebirth . . . not just to restore athletic games but to head a broader movement, where the Olympics exemplify 'education and culture' . . . Soutsos dreamed that the Games might foster among the participants a feeling of brotherhood, a lessening of hostilities. The rebirth of the Olympics, he wrote in his poetry and declaimed in his public talks, could be a force for peace . . . Soutsos had mainly patriotic motives, bordering on the nationalistic. The broader Olympic idea, with its emphasis on moral development and international competition, would come later.

The poet's initial suggestion was apparently noticed by Greek philanthropist Evangelis Zappas. In 1843, Zappas made a formal offer to King Otto to pay for the refounding of the Games. The king immediately called upon his foreign minister, Alexander Rizos Rangavis, to work with Zappas and implement his plan. Even with the king's backing, it wasn't until 1858 that a royal decree was declared providing for restoration of the Games, replete with horse races, track and field events, and prizes for the victors.

The "Olympia," as the Games were initially called, were held a year later in 1859, in Ludovikou Square in the heart of Athens. However, they were less than successful because spectators were not allowed. Eleven years later, in 1870, the Games resumed, this time in the magnificently restored Panathenaic Stadium, and they were restaged again in 1875 as part of the Olympia Industrial Exhibition. Competition was limited to the scions of noble families, who, as Young writes, "found it distasteful to compete with the working class"; no common men were allowed to compete. The twisted roots of the "myth of amateurism" can be detected here. Culturally, there was a great deal at stake. If an amateur—one who supposedly competed not for money but for the love of the sport—lost a race to a lower-class athlete, he lost his sense of class superiority.

However, this attitude only ensured that the Games "were of a very low standard," according to Dr. Varfi; along with the remarkably parallel outlook in the Olympic revival in Great Britain, it set the stage for the battles over the amateur status of athletes that have plagued the modern Olympic movement.

Despite these attempts that preceded his own efforts, the Baron deserves credit for delivering the first major public proposal for reviving the Games. At the Sorbonne in Paris, in 1892, Coubertin shared what he described as his boyhood dream—à la Heinrich Schliemann and the rediscovery of Troy—a modern Olympic Games. He wrote later: "[We] voted unanimously for the restoration of an idea that is two thousand years old . . . The Olympism of ancient Hellas has reemerged in the world after an eclipse of many centuries. I raise my glass to the Olympic idea which, like a ray of the all-powerful sun, has pierced the mists of the ages." Coubertin's story as founder of the modern Games fulfills the function of modern myth, condensing and compressing many stories into a single, immediately comprehensible tale. It is myth as the public dream, the sacred story that binds people together—in this case, to the public dream of a revitalized Europe.

For the next three and a half years, Coubertin traveled across Europe and to America to share his vision and raise the requisite funds to stage the Games that he hoped would "reinvigorate the dissipated youth of France." Serendipitously, the most enthusiastic response came from Greece, and Coubertin decided to stage the revival there.

With Greek pride at stake and the Greeks' love of home and hearth under the world's gaze, donations poured in from Greek peasants and millionaires alike. Finally, a philanthropist and entrepreneur, Georgias Averoff—"a modern Croesus," in the words of the famous American traveler Burton Holmes—took on the mantle of financing the Games.

LET THE GAMES RESUME

After the longest hiatus of any public event in history, and against the inspiring backdrop of the Parthenon, the Olympic Games were resurrected at 2:00 P.M. on Easter Sunday, April 6, 1896. More than one hundred thousand people crowded into the white marble Panathenaic Stadium in Athens to watch 311 athletes (three-quarters of them Greek) from fourteen nations compete in nine events. The American team, consisting mostly of college students organized by Princeton professor William Sloan, had arrived only the day before because of confusion between the traditional Greek and modern Western calendars. But they fared better than anyone had dared anticipate.

It had been a millennium and a half since the last victor had been crowned. The next one was about to earn his laurels—though for the first time he would not be Greek. James Connolly was a member of the Suffolk Athletic Club and a reluctant

Harvard dropout who had been forced to choose between college and the Olympics. Sixteen days after his decision, he found himself contending in the triple-jump competition in Athens. He was the last to jump, which allowed him the chance to note the mark of the leading jumper, Alexandre Tuffere, which was a mere 41 feet 8 inches, far shorter than his own best mark. Connolly confidently threw his cap down a few feet beyond the leading mark—and soared past even the cap with a winning mark of 44 feet, 11¾ inches. The stadium erupted with the ecstatic cry: *Nike, nike!* (Victory, victory!)

Other nations showed their mettle, such as Germany in gymnastics and wrestling, and France in cycling, where Paul Masson won three events. But the ebullient Americans dominated track and field.

According to Burton Holmes, who recorded his memoirs of the Athens Olympiad in *The Olympic Games: 1896*, the Greek spectators were exhilarated by the "enthusiasm and good sportsmanship" of the strangers from around the world who were competing for the laurels. Evincing the ancient Olympic spirit, they delighted in the display of excellence, whether in the contests for the finest odes composed in the ancient tongue or in the scientific training of the "American Invincibles" who won event after event. Most impressive to the Greeks was the chap from the Princeton team who upset their own national champion in the discus, Panagiotis Paraskevopolous.

"With the same undaunted spirit which has ever characterized the Anglo-Saxon race," writes Holmes, "Robert Garrett, of the Princeton team, took up the discus for the first time in his life and stood before the thronging thousands ready to do at least his best for the honor of the Orange and Black and the Stars and Stripes." On his third and last throw, "Garrett's discus, although launched by an unpracticed hand, had touched the earth just 7½ inches beyond that which the Greek [rival] had so artistically thrown." Despite being beaten at their own game, the Greeks were exemplary in defeat, saluting Garrett for the rest of the Games as the "American Hermes."

Nevertheless, as if the gods were smiling upon the epic patience of the Greeks, the best, in their view, was saved for last. In the ancient town of Marathon, twenty-five miles outside of Athens, seventeen runners, most of them Greek, gathered in the cobblestoned town square awaiting the start of the first official marathon.

The event was the brainchild of a French linguist and historian, Michel Breal, whose original idea was simply to stage a long distance race. Coubertin's interest was piqued, and he proposed to the Organizing Committee of the Athens Olympics a race to commemorate the epic tale of the lone runner, Phillipides (or "Phiddipides"), who had been dispatched to Athens to announce the Greek victory over the Persians on the plains of Marathon in 490 B.C.E. According to one tradition, before dying of exhaustion the weary runner managed to say, "Rejoice, we conquer!" But how closely aligned the martial and athletic spirits have always been is revealed in Stephen G. Miller's recent translation: "Be happy! We have won!"

With this mythic image in their hearts, the seventeen runners set off to recreate history—and to redeem Greek pride. Holmes reports, "The Greeks and barbarians are running with grim determination. They know that he who wins the race from Marathon will gain more than ephemeral honor, that the story of his victory will be recited to admiring generations long after the other contests have passed into oblivion."

The high jump competition was still underway as messengers on horseback and bicycle looped back and forth from the Marathon road to the Panathenian Stadium to report on the long distance race's progress. Prince George and Crown Prince Constantine leapt from the royal box and ran outside the stadium when word came "with the rapidity of lightning" that the first runner to cross the outer boulevards of the city was— *Elleen! Elleen!* (A Greek! A Greek!)

The news was epic—every Greek citizen's dream. A twenty-five-year-old shepherd, Spiridon Louis, "all dust and perspiration," appeared at the entrance of the stadium and staggered inside, right into the warm embrace of the exultant princes and a Russian grand duke. With the cheers of the crowd cascading down on them, the princes, the duke, and the pauper ran arm-in-arm to the finish line, while King George waved his royal cap, and Louis, using his last reserves of energy, bowed before the monarch.

After a wait of over fifteen hundred years, it only took two hours and fifty-eight minutes—the winning time of the marathon—for Greece to have a new champion. As a result, Holmes concludes, "the native cup of happiness is full."

Louis was the undisputed hero of the Games and the living embodiment of the timeless ideal of competing for a cause larger than oneself, either your country or history itself. In the spirit of their ancestors, the modern Greeks offered Louis a cornucopia of gifts: housing and monthly stipends, free meals, shoes, underwear, socks, and haircuts and shaves for life. Holmes reported that "A rich man gave him land in his native village, and a wealthy lady offered him the choice of a large sum of money— or a kiss." The simple peasant's response to all the munificent offers is the stuff of modern myth. Unaffected by the fervor over his victory, in the end all he received was the traditional crown of wild olive leaves from Olympia and the one prize he requested—a horse and cart to help him transport water to his village. Then he retired to his village and never raced again.

Many Olympic scholars credit Spiridon Louis's stout-hearted performance with maintaining interest in the Games during their early, stutter-stepping years, for his courageous achievement was interpreted as evidence of a direct lineage between the ancient and modern Games. The Greeks' volcanic outpouring of love for one of their own recalls the beauty of the ancient epitaph to a champion found on an anonymous ancient Greek tomb:

> I grew from the earth.
> I flourished in my day.
> I am earth again.

Forty years after his victory, the valiant runner was invited by the Nazis to the opening ceremonies of the 1936 Berlin Games in an effort to glamorize them or at least gain some credibility. In Leni Riefenstahl's classic film, *Olympia,* the mustachioed marathoner can be seen for a few fleeting seconds, dressed in traditional Greek costume for the Games' opening procession. He appears blissfully unaware of the manipulation of his story but keenly proud of his stature in the eyes of his fellow athletes around the world.

As with the names of all immortal characters, his name lives on. To this day, the Greek expression *egine Louise* suggests somebody just "became Louis"—ran quickly.

GODS, GAMES, AND GUTS

The Roots of Agony and Ecstasy

"Come along, sir, have a try at the games yourself,
if you have any skill. Sport is the best way to fame
for any man alive—what you can do
with your arms and legs."

—HOMER, *Odyssey*

My country did not send me to Mexico City to start the race. They sent me to finish the race.

—JOHN STEPHEN AKHWAR,
Tanzanian marathoner

———————— ✸ ————————

In 420 B.C.E., the Olympic champion in the sprint-race, a runner named Exaenetus, returned home to Akragas, in present-day Sicily, and was given the traditional victor's welcome. Three hundred chariots were waiting for him, each one pulled by two white horses and driven by a leading citizen. Together they accompanied the great runner, draped in royal purple, into the city—but not through the gates. Instead, they escorted him through a great gap in the wall where the stones had been pulled down in his honor. Once inside, he was paraded through the streets and showered with fresh flowers to the tumultuous sound of cheering and weeping. Later that night a banquet was held in his honor. Every detail of his journey was recounted, songs were sung and poems recited, and plans were made for a bronze statue of him to be erected in the center of the city.

The fame of an Olympic champion didn't end even with his descent into the land of the shades. "In many cases," writes Jane Harrison in *Themis*, "he was worshipped after death, as a hero;

47

not because he was a successful athlete, but because he had once been an incarnate god."

Considering how vital walls were for a city's protection during that era of brutal warfare, knocking a hole in one was a risky act; but as ritual, it was rich with symbolic power. "It seems likely that this custom," writes Ludwig Drees in *Olympia,* "derived from the early period of the festival when the victor assumed the identity of the god and consequently would have been entitled to a private entrance." By knocking down a wall in honor of their conquering heroes, citizens across the ancient Greek world were acknowledging their admiration for superhuman achievement, as well as basking in the heroes' glory. The custom was also a rather sly way of saying, "Who needs walls when a giant among men dwells among us?"

On the collective level, the tradition of tumbling down walls also echoed the idealism of the times. For the hope of the ancient Games was that the inspiring spectacle of young warrior-athletes competing peacefully might break down walls of suspicion and enmity between rival city-states, who were rarely on peaceful terms with each other. The sanctuary's inviolate status provided a rare opportunity to display what all Greeks had in common—religion, language, and athletics—and perhaps inspire the diplomats who crowded around the temples and stadium.

Many centuries and Games later, in the summer of 1952, seventy thousand people in the Helsinki Olympic Stadium waited hours in a steady rain for the arrival of the final torchbearer. When the runner at last appeared, he was greeted by silence. At first, no one recognized the balding, unsmiling, fifty-five-year-old man who carried the Olympic flame. But as he ran the final lap his long stride and stoic bearing began to look hauntingly familiar: he was none other than their own legendary long distance runner Paavo Nurmi, "the greatest of all Finnish gods," as one Olympic historian has described him.

Paavo Nurmi lights the cauldron at the 1952 Helsinki Games.
His early regimen, he explained to the press, had included
racing the mail train near his home in Turku, Finland.

Over the course of three Olympiads, Nurmi had competed
in twelve races and earned twelve medals, including nine golds—
the most by any male athlete other than standing jumper Ray
Ewry—and had broken world records in every distance he ever
ran. All this was in the spectators' hearts and minds as they
thundered applause for their native son—who ran with his characteristic deep focus, impervious as always to their hero worship.

When Nurmi had completed his single lap around the stadium, he jogged to the ceremonial cauldron set in the infield and

lit the Olympic flame, igniting further fireworks of emotion throughout the stadium. The joyous welcome home would have made the citizens of Akragas proud.

Another story about Paavo Nurmi further evokes the Games' ideal spirit. I first heard about it my freshman year in college, at the University of Detroit, while working out with the cross-country team. I can still see in my mind's eye the other runners shaking their heads in near disbelief. The story goes that during the qualifying round for the 3,000-meter steeplechase at the 1928 Olympics in Amsterdam, Nurmi tripped over the first hurdle and fell into the water jump. One of his rivals, French runner Lucien Duquesne, stopped and helped him get back on his feet and into the race. Nurmi was so grateful for the unexpected gesture that he refused to surge on ahead. Instead, he ran shoulder to shoulder, like a brother in arms, with Duquesne for the rest of the race. Together, they crossed the finish line.

In the finals Nurmi won the silver medal in what turned out to be his last Olympics race. Shortly after, the International Olympic Committee disqualified him from the 1932 Los Angeles Games. They were concerned about his violations of "amateurism," defined as engaging in "quasiprofessional activities." The decision deeply embittered Nurmi, who retreated into near-seclusion, and angered the people of Finland toward the entire Olympic movement.

But twenty-four years after the tragic ban, the people spoke with their hearts and souls. The outpouring of raw emotion for Nurmi that rainy day in Helsinki went beyond the fact that he had set numerous world records and won medals. So it is always with our athletic heroes. In the end it is our love for them that matters—our appreciation for their sacrifices, their beauty, their strength, and their courage. This love is what endures.

These two legendary runners, Exaenetus and Nurmi, are linked across the centuries by their ability to run like gods but also by the fiery devotion of their fans. Just as the Olympic torch is passed from hand to hand, so too can the spirit of the inspired athlete be passed along to those in the stands—or to those down the long road of history who hear about them and still feel the telltale shiver of awe and wonder.

Why do runners hold such a high place in our pantheon of heroes? Why are godlike qualities attributed to the great ones? As a matter of fact, why do we run at all—first freely, then competitively, in contests and games?

THE RACE OF LIFE

"Race ya!" I heard some young boys yell at my seven-year-old son, Jack, at a local park recently. When I asked him afterward why he immediately dashed off with them, Jack said, "For the fun of it, Papa!" Later in the week, I asked a woman friend who has run marathons for years why she runs. She said, "To take the edge off. It's been the one place in my life where I could ever be alone with my own thoughts." Her soulful response reminded me of a comment by one of Nurmi's childhood friends: "Running was [his] attempt at finding real life."

The legendary Roger Bannister, the first man to break four minutes in the mile, explained that his career was rooted in recognition of running's intangible, spiritual dimension. "Whether we like it or not, the four-minute mile had become rather like an Everest—a challenge to the human spirit."

Another athlete who has confronted the spiritual challenge in sports is Australian aborigine runner Cathy Freeman, who won the 400-meter race at the Sydney 2000 Games. She relishes talking about her girlhood ritual of writing the words *Olympic champion* on the chalkboard at her school. For her, running was more than personal accomplishment; it was a way to bring dignity to her people.

Ultra-marathoner, biologist, and author Bernd Heinrich has also mused over the deeper motivations that drive athletes. In *Why We Run* he writes that human beings run because in the very depths of our being—in our DNA or in our soul—we are chasing down "dream antelopes." According to this playful but scientifically sound theory, millions of years of running after wild game—such as antelope—has infused us with a primal urge to reenact the ancient chase. Peter Nabakov recounts in *Indian Running* how many Native American tribes selected boys to run down wild animals—a dazzlingly dangerous adventure. Other tribes encouraged adults to run hundreds of miles as part of a sacred pilgrimage, while offering up their pain and suffering to the gods.

Warrior-adventurer-philosopher George Leonard, in *The Ultimate Athlete*, concurs: "The prehistoric hunters were among the greatest runners the planet has known. Each of us still owns some fragment from the ruins of that ancient glory." He adds, "What we run for we shall never reach, and that is the heart and the glory of it. In the end, running is its own reward. It can never be justified. We run for the sake of running, nothing more."

Traditionally, descriptions of Olympic runners have been on the rhapsodic side, such as the tale of fleet-footed Lacas, said to run so swiftly that he left no prints behind in the sand. But as much as they valued success, there is some evidence, especially in the great satires, that the Greeks disdained anything less. The epigramist Lucillius told a story about a long distance runner named Marcus who ran one race so slowly that he was mistaken for a statue before he even entered the stadium. The caretakers could not tell he was still "running," so they locked the gates at day's end with Marcus still on the track. When the stadium was reopened the next morning, poor Marcus had still not finished.

To the scientist, philosopher, historian, and athlete we run *by instinct*, we are natural-born runners. We run because we long to be carried away. When asked how he ran so fast, the immortal Jesse Owens, winner of four gold medals at the Berlin Games, replied, "I let my feet spend as little time on the ground as possible. From the air, fast down, and from the ground, fast up. My foot is only a fraction of the time on the track."

But if playing and running are such "pure" pleasures, why push our luck and take them to the next level to compete and contest against others? Why isn't it enough to run, jump, throw, or play by and for ourselves? What is the difference between play and competition?

AT PLAY IN THE FIELDS OF THE GODS

"Time is a child playing," wrote the classical sage Heraclitus, "moving counters on a game-board: the kingdom belongs to a child." The metaphor is powerfully accurate, reflecting the way that play allows children to practice their upcoming roles as adults by exercising their imagination, or by simply exulting in the freedom of movement. As children know, play has no goal other than itself—only the reverie that comes from living purely in the moment. The beauty of play is its spontaneity, the reveling in the body's possibilities and the joy of natural learning. Yet play is crucial not only to the individual child but to the childhood of the human species.

Sports historian Allan Guttman offers a concise set of distinctions. He suggests that play is spontaneous activity, while games are organized play, contests are competitive games, and sports are physical contests. The impulse for *evolution* from one level to another is enigmatic. Sportswriter Frank Deford offers a partial explanation for this development in a *National Geographic* essay on the 1960 Rome Olympics: "The wellspring of sport is the human impulse to turn work, warfare—indeed, all of life— into games."

Psychiatrist and play expert Stuart Brown agrees whole-heartedly that play is fundamental and a primary engine of evolution. "My first inclination," he told me in a recent interview, "is to ground play and games in the wondrous world of animal play and the mysteries of self-organizing systems. Grace and agility, endurance and perseverance, optimism and confidence are grounded in that special state of being that is hard to define but recognizable as *play*. The Olympic Games are a manifestation of an evolved play-game cooperative festival that has its heritage in 100 million years of ancestral trial and error. While not everyone is an Olympic-level athlete, we are all players, animals and humans alike. The utter joyous absorption of the true player in his or her play-art has its parallels in the quest for excellence in body, mind, and spirit."

Brown's associate in play research, Bob Fagan, an expert in animal play and bear behavior, believes play has profound long-term benefits: "Play is a rehearsal for the challenges and ambiguities of life."

Dutch author Johan Huizinga, in the classic *Homo Ludens* (Man the Player), writes, "In play . . . the antithetical and ago-nistic basis of civilization is given from the start, for play is older and more original than civilization . . . Latin was right in calling the sacred contests by the simple word 'play,' because it express-es as purely as possible the unique nature of this civilizing force."

Huizinga maintains that though the Greeks had no single wide-ranging word for play, their entire universe was imbued with *agonistic* activities, the "play-spirit." From the gods' roll of the dice to determine a person's "lot in life," or "destiny," to the omnipresence of contests, the play-function was in constant use.

© IOC/Olympic Museum Collections

At the 1976 Montreal Games, fourteen-year-old gymnast Nadia
Comaneci stunned the athletic world with seven perfect scores.

Play's existential associations have their roots in the very
origins of the word, which derives from two sources. The Anglo-
Saxon *plegan* means "to exercise, make brisk or rapid movement
or gestures, a grasp of the hands, clapping, playing on a musical
instrument and all kinds of bodily movement." The Old Dutch
pleien means "to leap for" or "dance." The oldest associations of
this venerable word describe sacred acts in ceremonial rites and

the celebrating of festivals, which are borne out in the translation's suggestions of joy, music, and creative movement. Thus, through the marvels of word archaeology we discover a treasure in the idea of play and its practice: play is both instinctual and existential. It allows us to seize the moment and celebrate life while defying the gravity of convention by juggling with the balls of reality. Existentially, play brings us home to what Buddhists call "the miracle of the present moment." Its ecstatic nature reminds us at every moment that we need not be victims of fate—or, as we would say today, of our genetic makeup. It constantly reveals new possibilities, which is why the German Romantic poet Novalis said, "Play is experimenting with chance." In this delightful way we arrive at play's sacred character—the revelation through music, drama, law, ritual, poetry, and games that to *play* at the *meaning of life* is, paradoxically, to take it most seriously.

Hence, we play with ideas, engage in love-play during "the jewel of all games," play with words in poetry, play with the gods in religion. The opposite, Huizinga points out, is being in *earnest*, a word that originally meant "strife" or "struggle." To paraphrase Oscar Wilde, the importance of being playful is in dramatic contrast to the importance of being earnest.

In this light, the genius of the Greek *agon,* or "contest," was the way it manifested the dream of reconciliation between the inevitability of strife—which is the father of everything, according to Heraclitus—and the desire to play *enthusiastically,* which means you are "filled with the gods." The tension that links together athletics, drama, and poetry is the strife that the protagonist, or *agoniste*—the actor or the athlete—must overcome.

"The contest reigned supreme as the life-principle," says Huizinga. "The sacred character of the *agon* was everywhere. Greeks used to stage contests in anything that offered the barest possibility of a fight." Whether competing in poetry, riddle-solving, or drinking, the sacred dimension was always present, for it was believed that mortal play amused the immortals. "Play is a thing in itself," Huizinga concludes, and it belongs to a higher realm than seriousness. "For seriousness seeks to exclude play, whereas play can very well include seriousness."

It is in the contest that one can win glory, honor, and esteem—three highly charged values in ancient Greek culture.

"No doubt," Huizinga writes, "the few centuries of Greek history when the contest reigned supreme as the life-principle of society also saw the rise of the great sacred games which united all Hellas at Olympia, on the Isthmus [Corinth], at Delphi and Nemea; but the fact remained that the spirit of the contest dominated Hellenic culture both before those centuries, and after."

This competitive spirit dates back to Homer's epic poems, where his heroes and warriors are described as "athletes and not merchants," and desiring "always to be the first and to surpass others." Ever after, competition and contests ranged widely in ancient Greek culture, from the public forum, the battlefield, and the courts to contests in beauty, drinking, music, singing, or riddle-solving. What was being contested always had to do with strength, beauty, wit, wisdom, or wealth.

"What then is the right way of living?" Plato writes in the *Laws*; and he supplies the answer: "Life must be lived as play, playing certain games, making sacrifices, singing and dancing, and then a man will propitiate the gods and defend himself against his enemies and win in the contest." In this passage Plato is underlining the spiritual dimension of play, the feeling in the midst of it that the gods are near and, when play metamorphoses into games, that something divine is at work. In *God and Games*, David L. Miller writes, "These dimensions of play may be thought of as a culmination of the evolution of consciousness..." To reanimate our lives, he writes, "we should work as if at play" and practice a "theology of play."

For the Dutch historian of religion Gerardus Van Der Leeuw, the realm of play and the arena of the game are powerful modern metaphors. They act as constant reminders that we are in the middle of sacred drama and that we need not to take ourselves so seriously. "The meeting of God with man, of man with God, is holy play, *sacer ludi*," he writes in *Sacred and Profane Beauty: The Holy in Art*. "For this reason, the game points beyond itself: downward, to the simple ordinary rhythm of life; upward, to the highest form of existence."

One of the poet laureates of sports in our time was Harvard scholar and baseball commissioner the late A. Bart Giamatti, who wrote extensively about the modern spirit of play. In *Take Time for Paradise*, he touches upon athletic competition's spiritual dimension: "I believe we played games, and watched games, to imitate the gods, to become godlike in our worship of each other and, through those moments of transmutation, to know for an instant what the gods know." At the end of the day, this is what enchants us, casts a spell over us, and provides us with those elusive moments that transcend displays of skill, technique, or brute strength and grant us a vision.

Giamatti continues: "So games, contests, sports reiterate the purpose of freedom every time they are enacted—the purpose being to show us how to be free and to be complete, connected, unimpeded and integrated, all at once. That is the role of leisure, and if leisure were a god, rather than Aristotle's version of the highest human state, sport would be a constant reminder—not a faded remnant—of that transcendent or sacred being . . . As our forebears did, we remind ourselves through sport of what, here on earth, is our noblest hope. Through sport, we re-create our daily portion of freedom, in public."

To value the transcendent moments more than the tallying of medals on the scoreboard and thus revive competition's spiritual dimension is the Olympic challenge that lies before us.

THE MYTHOPOETICS
OF SPORTS

"In the beginning," writes Rudolph Brasch in *How Did Sports Begin?* "[sport] was a religious cult and a preparation for life. Its roots were in man's desire to gain victory over foes seen and unseen, to influence the forces of nature, and to promote fertility among his crops and cattle."

Once these primary needs were met, Brasch continues, the exhilaration of early sporting activities was carried on in the form of free play or games. What began as essential training for hunting or warfare became mere diversion or amusement, though in its own unique way sport is just as essential to our well-being as the original need to feed or protect ourselves.

"In our time millions of people," Brasch writes, "whether spectators or participants, amateurs or professionals, are carried away by the sport they love from the cares of their daily toil, their anxieties and frustrations, to a world of relaxation and emulation, excitement and thrill." Thus sports are not an avoidance of life but an embrace of it in all its complexities, a conscious transformation of the battle of life into the game of life.

The ancient Greeks described competition as the fruit of a pivotal moment in prehistory. The biographer Plutarch chronicled the situation this way: "In the ruthless times before athletics, it appears that at that time there were men who, for deftness of hand, speed of legs, and strength of muscles, transcended normal human nature and were tireless. They never used their physical capacities to do good or to help others, but reveled in their own brutal arrogance and enjoyed exploiting their strength to commit savage, ferocious deeds, conquering, ill-treating, and murdering whosoever fell into their hands."

"It is Theseus and Herakles," writes Roberto Calasso, citing Plutarch, "who first use force to a different end than that of merely crushing their opponents. They become 'athletes on behalf of men.' And, rather than strength itself, what they care about is the art of applying it: 'Theseus invented the art of wrestling, and later teaching of the sport took the basic moves from him. Before Theseus, it was merely a question of height and brute force.'"

The Western world since the fall of the Roman empire has been marked by a Manichaean suspicion of the physical. The ideal education has been intellectual and spiritual, with only begrudging attention given to the balance of mind, body, and soul that the ancient Greeks sought. It was not until the work of eighteenth- and nineteenth-century philosopher-poets like Friedrich von Schiller and Greek scholar Thomas Arnold of Rugby that play and games once again earned their rightful place in the well-rounded education. Schiller wrote incisively about art, beauty, freedom, and spirit—the thread that ties them together being the beauty born in play. For Schiller, play is the link between the inner world of reverie and the outer world of concrete things. Arnold was the first educator in modern times to advocate games as an indispensable part of school life. Coubertin made the pilgrimage to the Rugby school, in England, and later on in life praised Arnold for creating the ideal athletic atmosphere for young students.

"Nobility of spirit is the grace—or ability—to play," writes Joseph Campbell in *The Masks of God*, "whether in heaven or on earth. And this, I take it, this *noblesse oblige*, which has always been the quality of aristocracy, was precisely the virtue (*arete*) of the Greek poets, artists, and philosophers, for whom the gods were true as poetry is true."

Play is noble, spirited, graceful, and virtuous: it is through play's "as if" leap of faith that we enter another world and realize ecstatic possibilities for ourselves we wouldn't discover otherwise. The nature of that other world is at once nostalgic, as suggested by all the references to "home" in sports, and ideal-istic, as revealed in the innocent longing for sheer *fun,* which inexplicably has the power to renew our spirits, even to "recre-ate" us. The mythopoetics of sports declare that we can best comprehend the world through awe and wonder, a viewpoint possible only with a play-full attitude towards life.

When I interviewed Campbell in Honolulu in the spring of 1985, during the making of the documentary film, *The Hero's Journey,* he was immensely pleased that I wanted to talk about the mythic significance of sports. As one of the fastest half-milers in his day—he came within one second of the world record in his victory at the Penn Relays—he was more than eager to talk about the mythic function of athletics.

"Young men are testosterone machines," Campbell told me emphatically. "You have to challenge all the energy or they'll burn your cities down. I don't know what I would have done without athletics when I was a young man. It gave me discipline for a lifetime. I still swim forty-four laps a day, meditating on a different tarot card during each lap."

Campbell paused, as if perusing a mental scrapbook of arti-cles from his illustrious track career. Then he smiled and added, "I still think of my running career every time I lecture." His lec-tures were "the equivalent of a half-mile race, and boy, I'll tell you, they're both tough. Life's tough. Running taught me how to pace myself in everything I've done in my life. It takes real guts to make your way through this world. The discipline you learn in sports can give you that."

Shortly after our interview, Campbell told Michael Toms, of New Dimensions radio, about watching a track meet on televi-sion: "It was the first such meet I had beheld since I myself had been a competitor back in the middle twenties—a lapse of about forty years, during all of which time I had paid no attention to the sport, mainly because it aroused in me more emotion than I wanted to have to control. What I chanced upon was a mile race of six glorious runners. What a really beautiful thing . . . When the game is played really seriously . . . and confronts directly the honest challenge of the field, we have *form* and we have it in grand style."

I thought of Campbell's reflections on the sporting life recently when I heard Lance Armstrong interviewed on television. The four-time Tour de France and Olympic medal winner is now as famous for having survived testicular and brain cancer as he is for his racing prowess. What's his secret? He says, "If I don't suffer a little every day, I feel guilty." That is, he needs to feel that he has beaten the odds time after time.

Why does so much emotion surface when we recall the races of our youth? Why do we love the struggle? Is it pathological, as some psychologists insist, or do great athletes know something the rest of us have forgotten—or rejected?

"Whenever their lives were set aflame," writes Roberto Calasso, "through desire or suffering, or even reflection, the Homeric heroes knew that a god was at work."

THE ROOTS OF
OUR AGONY AND ECSTASY

Leave it to a poet—the ancient Greek Pindar—to say, "The word outlives the deed." Though literature tends to outlive the people who write it, if we look close enough we can still see the deeds living inside the histories of the words. So, also the often inexplicably powerful response we feel in the heat of competition, whether as athletes or spectators, is at least partially expressed in the compacted meaning of the words we use to describe the athletic experience.

Consider the marvels of the puzzle-box of words used in the wide world of *sports*—a word that derives from the Latin *des-porto*, meaning "carry away." Of course, getting "carried away" is the thing our parents and teachers said we shouldn't do. Despite their warnings, most of us indeed play or watch sports to get carried away as often as possible from the workaday life. We love to lose ourselves, at least temporarily, and it is this sense of "transport," a product of physical exertion, that rejuvenates athletes.

Strictly speaking, an athlete is someone who competes for a prize in public games. Our word *athlete* comes from the Greek *athlon*, meaning a prize won in a game. The English word *game* derives from a wonderful old Danish word *gammen*, which refers to mirth or merriment. The prize can also be won in a contest, which in Greek was *agon*, the root of our word *agony*. To train or compete is agony; yet only agony leads to ecstasy. Today many athletes boast "No pain, no gain"—and believe they invented the idea. But as early as the fourth century B.C.E., at least one spectator in the gymnasium was so in awe of the athletes' ability to endure that he wrote, "In their pain is their fame."

The game is worth the pain because the ecstasy is worth the agony. If you go deep enough into agony you find the real meaning of *ecstasy*, from the Greek *exstasis*, which denotes "being beside yourself"—what we now call being "in the zone," "in the bubble," or "in the flow." The *real* contest is a test of our spirit, and if played seriously it leads us to a place beyond our ordinary selves. The ecstatic side of sports is above and beyond the advertised prize of the contest; it offers the athlete a momentary experience of the rapturous and dramatic.

The Greeks were acutely aware of these connections. Their word for "actor" was *agonistes*, which was also the word for "competitor." To them, athlete and actor were kindred spirits. Each played in a drama in which occurred an unfolding of fate or destiny, a symbolic life and death. There's good reason why sports are called a *past*-time—they are supposed to take us outside and beyond ourselves, lift us up so we transcend everyday life.

"It's that shudder out of time," writes adventurer-poet Diane Ackerman in *Deep Play*, "the central moment in so many sports, that one often feels, and perhaps becomes addicted to, while doing something dangerous . . . the fear of leaning into nothingness."

This risk taking has been at the heart of the attraction of the sporting life from the very beginning. As David C. Young writes, "In the readiness of adult men to run the naked risk of public dishonor for the chance to achieve distinction, there we find what separated Greeks from all other people."

Risking everything by training hard for years, then exposing themselves to possible defeat, even humiliation, yet achieving some form of distinction is *still* what separates the Olympic athlete from all others. This is the mysterious source of joy for them—and often for us.

TO STRIVE, TO SEEK, AND NOT TO YIELD

As the Irish are fond of saying, memory is a merciful editor. Swiss psychologist C. G. Jung went so far as to say that every attempt at turning memory into narrative is mythological. Such is the case with one of my favorite stories from ancient times, the tale of Glaucus of Carystus, in Euboea, the Olympic boxing victor in 520 B.C.E.

The legend has it that young Glaucus was the son of a farmer. One day while Glaucus was working in the field, the plowshare came loose from the plow. Not having any tools nearby, Glaucus knocked it back into its socket with his stone-hard bare fist, a colossal feat his father happened to notice.

Encouraged by his father, Glaucus went to Olympia and won his first few bouts—but also lost a few teeth and a lot of blood. By the last match he was exhausted and seriously wounded. It is said that the spectators and his trainer expected him at any point to lift his forefinger in the traditional gesture of surrender. But at the moment of truth—when the goddess of victory, Nike, or the god of sacred time, Kairos, were known to appear—Glaucus's father (or, in one account, his trainer) suddenly bellowed, "My boy, remember the plowshare!"

As if prefiguring Muhammad Ali's remarkable comeback in the "thrilla in Manila" fight, Glaucus seized the moment and dug down deep within himself for one last surge of strength and courage. He rose up and walloped his rival on the head as hard as he had hit the plowshare—and the contest was over.

What are we to make out of such a tale?

As with many Olympic stories, both ancient and modern, the tale of Glaucus is instructive on many levels. It has survived the exigencies of time not because it glamorizes brutality but because it mythologizes—makes a sacred story out of—the otherwise ineffable way human beings discover their secret strength in a moment of truth.

Strength, however, isn't always corporeal; sometimes it is spiritual, as echoed in the words of Mohandas Gandhi: "Strength does not come from physical strength. It comes from an indomitable will."

The story of Jesse Owens in the 1936 Berlin Games has become enshrined as one of our modern sports myths, an inspirational story close to my own heart. I remember the first time I heard his name. It was the late 1960s, and our high school track team was competing at the University of Michigan track in Ann Arbor. As part of his pep talk, our coach, Mr. Leonard Natkowski, informed us we should feel honored because we were about to run on the same track where Jesse Owens had raced in the Big Ten Championships. That was the day, May 25, 1935, when he broke three world records and tied a fourth—in a span of seventy minutes.

There's a fine line between inspiration and intimidation, but I do recall how my feet prickled in my track shoes that afternoon, as if the track itself was sacred ground. That day I ran my fastest 440-yard dash ever and broke my own long jump record. A few years later, while wandering around Berlin, I read about Owens's magnificent performance there in the 1936 Games and felt an uncanny connection with him; I was filled with what James Joyce calls "a riot of emotion."

The 1936 Berlin Olympics were part of Hitler's grandiose plan to prove to the world the superiority of the "Aryan" people. But Jesse Owens and a handful of other foreign athletes upstaged his plans. Owens won the hearts of his teammates but also the affection of the German crowd by winning gold medals in the 100-meter dash, the 200-meter dash, the 400-meter relay, and the long jump. This feat made him the first American in the annals of Olympic history to win four golds in one Olympiad. That's the overstory. The understory, the stuff of myth, is how he won the gold in the long jump—which, as he later said, made the other victories possible.

Because he was the world-record holder at 26 feet, 8¼ inches (which he had set in Ann Arbor), Owens was heavily favored to win. But, as sportswriter Ron Fimrite reports, "Under the baleful gaze of Adolf Hitler, he fouled on the first two jumps [and] had one chance remaining to qualify for the finals."

Owens said later, "I fought, I fought harder . . . but one cell at a time, panic crept into my body, taking me over." Owens was agonizing over what to do with his last jump when he was approached by one of his rivals, Germany's Luz Long. Although he was the very epitome of the pure Aryan youth—a tall, blond, and blue-eyed athlete—Long was completely unsympathetic with the vainglorious theories of Nazi superiority. While the German officials watched, Long blithely befriended Owens.

"What's eating you?" he asked his African-American opponent. "You should be able to qualify with your eyes closed." Knowing that the qualifying distance was only 23 feet, 5½ inches, Long deftly recommended that Owens simply mark a spot a few inches *before* the wooden takeoff board and jump from there. Long even offered to mark the spot with his towel. Owens smiled and thanked him and easily qualified on his next jump. Later that day, after five jumps and at 25 feet, 10 inches, Owens was tied, ironically, with Long, who was staging the greatest performance of his own career. On his final jump, inspired by his new friend's gesture of brotherhood, Owens leapt 26 feet, 5½ inches—surpassing Long and shattering the Olympic record.

The first to congratulate him was Long, who lifted Owens's arm high in the sky. "I had gone farther than Luz," Owens wrote in his autobiography. "I had set a new Olympic record. I had jumped farther than any man on earth. Luz didn't let go of my arm. He lifted it up—as he had lifted me in a different way a few days before—and led me away from the pit and toward the crowd. 'Jazze Owens!' he shouted. 'Jazze Owens!' Some people in the crowd responded, 'Jazze Owens!' They were cheering me. But only I knew who they were really cheering. I lifted Luz Long's arm.

"'Luz Long!' I yelled at the top of my lungs. 'Luz Long! Luz Long!'"

Years later, Owens said, "In a more important way...*he* was the winner. He had done his best—and without him I never could have done my best. Luz truly showed the spirit of the Olympics...You can melt down all the medals and cups I have and they would be plating on the 24-carat friendship I felt for Long at that moment."

The paragon of grace and courage, American track star Jesse Owens shares a moment with his newfound friend, the brilliant German long jumper, Luz Long, at the 1936 Berlin Games.

Owens was filmed on the victory stand, grinning underneath the olive leaf crown and showing a flash of true Olympic spirit as he said simply, "Thanks for the grand competition."

After the Olympics Owens quickly turned professional because, as he said at the time, "I had four gold medals, but you can't eat four gold medals." He spent the last years of life on the inspirational lecture circuit, a lifework that proved more rewarding than his world records, which have long since been broken.

"Grown men stop me on the street, and say, 'Mr. Owens, I heard you talk fifteen years ago in Minneapolis. I'll never forget that speech.' And I think to myself, that man probably has children of his own now. And maybe, maybe, he remembers a specific point I made. Maybe he is passing that point on to his own son just as I said it. And then I think—that's immortality. You are *immortal* if your ideas are being passed from a father to a son to his son and on and on and on."

THE SPIRIT OF
THE UNDERDOG

As Michael Novak writes in *The Joy of Sports*, "Sports are creations of the human spirit, arenas of the human spirit, witnesses to the human spirit, instructors of the human spirit."

In this rhythmic sentence he captures the overarching function of the spirit that both creates and is created by those who play games at the highest imaginable level. Talent is admired, but spirit is embraced. Spirit is what helps you rise above yourself, and who doesn't want to improve themselves? If the athlete is not just gifted but inspired, the spirit that infuses her can inspire others. And for this she is loved.

In December, 1999, *Sports Illustrated* voted Mildred "Babe" Didrikson the greatest female athlete of the twentieth century. Her biographer describes her as admired by average Americans who "appreciated her guts in taking what was due her." Friends nicknamed her "Babe" after the beloved baseball slugger Babe Ruth because she was considered his female equivalent as the greatest athlete of the day. She hailed from dirt-poor roots and rose to the top of the world, excelling at running, jumping, swimming, ball playing of every kind, golf, and several track and field sports.

At seventeen, Babe became, as Susan Wels writes in *The Olympic Spirit,* "the hands-down queen of the Los Angeles Olympic Games . . . who personally embodied the Olympic motto 'Faster, Higher, Stronger.'" Didrikson earned two Olympic gold medals: her first in the javelin with a toss of 143 feet, 4 inches, and her second, which also set a world record, in the 80-meter hurdles. She just missed a third in the high jump when she tied Jean Shiley at 5 feet, 5¼ inches but lost in the runoff for her headfirst dive over the bar, which was ruled illegal. Underscoring her reputation as the greatest athlete of her time, she had qualified for two other events, but the rules of the day stipulated she could only compete in three. "I could have won a medal in five events if they'd let me," she grinned later.

© IOC/Olympic Museum Collections

The sublime Babe Didrikson (second from the right) on her way to victory in the 80-meter hurdles at the women's AAU track and field championships, Northwestern University, 1932.

Beloved sportswriter Grantland Rice described Didrikson as "the most flawless section of muscle harmony, of complete mental and physical coordination the world of sports has ever known." She injected an element of tricksterlike playfulness into women's athletics, along with the kind of spirited confidence that Muhammad Ali would later bring to boxing—a trait that earned her as much envy as admiration.

In later life, she took her talents to the vaudeville stage, where she rode horses and played harmonica, and joined a traveling all-women Jewish baseball team, the House of David, that played two hundred games a year. "Boy, don't you wish men could hit a ball like that?" she remarked after one game. When asked, after her superb performance at the Los Angeles Games, if there was anything she didn't play, Babe replied laconically, "I don't play with dolls."

SHORTHAND FOR STRUGGLE

Six decades later, in one of the defining moments of the 1996 Summer Olympics in Atlanta, another young woman, Kerri Strug, "a most unlikely hero," as *Sports Illustrated* described her, captured the world's heart with a courageous victory.

In the final round of the gymnastics team competition all looked lost for the Americans. Their coach, Bela Karolyi, told them that everything depended on Strug's last vault—that she needed at least a 9.6 score to fend off the Russians.

On her first vault, the four-foot nine-inch, eighty-five-pound gymnast landed on her heels and fell backwards, twisting her ankle. "Shake it out," bellowed her coach. Strug was numb with pain and asked quietly, "Do I have to do this again?" She didn't have to wait for an answer. Gamely, she took to the mat and sprinted down the runway, chanting to herself, "I will, I will, I will!" and soared over the horse—then landed with full weight on her severely sprained ankle. She winced with pain as she hopped on her one good foot and raised her arms in triumph for a few seconds before falling to the mat, but the trace of a smile could be seen on her face. She knew she had nailed the landing.

The next day, the photograph of Karolyi carrying the wisp of a girl to the victory stand was beamed across the world, as was another stirring but unusual photo. It showed the three medal-winners from the team gymnastics competition, but from the shoulders down. The two women who flanked Kerri Strug

© IOC/Olympic Museum Collections

Winner of the 1996 Olympic Spirit Award, gymnast Kerri Strug is carried to the award platform by her coach, Bela Karolyi, after her courageous vault on a sprained ankle.

stood on strong, healthy legs, while she gingerly balanced on her one good leg. Her other leg was half-cocked, the sprained ankle wrapped tightly in a cast.

Gazing at photographs of Strug's moments of agony and ecstasy, I recalled the loving inscription found on the pedestal of a long-lost statue at Olympia: "I, Nikophiolos, put up this statue in Parian marble in honor of my beautiful sister Kikegora, who won the girl's race."

As fate would have it, Coach Karolyi had miscounted the team score. The U.S. team would have claimed the gold without the 9.712 score earned by Kerri. But the spirit of her performance—the way she transformed pain into triumph before our very eyes—embodies what is best about the Olympics.

In that tenuous moment, when victory hung on a thread, she showed us strength and beauty, courage and grace, and an almost unfathomable desire to excel. To rise to this level takes courage, skill, and fortitude, a task so agonizing for mere mortals that it inspired an old wag named Eli Mygatt to coin the phrase: "God, give me guts."

THE
SACRED FESTIVAL

---❋---

CELEBRATION OF
THE CONTEST

*The whole of humanity now aspires to this harmony.
The prestige and fame of the Olympic ideal at a world level
is confirmation enough of this. It is therefore, incumbent
upon us to respond to the need to restore the movement
to its Greek roots and revive the ancient Athenian spirit.*

—DIMITRIS L. AVRAMOPOULOS,
Mayor of Athens

If the Olympic Games were being held now you would be able to see for yourself why we attach so much importance to athletics. No one can describe in mere words the extraordinary . . . pleasure derived from them and which you yourself would enjoy if you were seated among the spectators feasting your eyes on the prowess and stamina of the athletes, the power of their bodies, their invincible strength, their beauty, courage, incredible dexterity and skills.

—LUCIAN,
second century B.C.E.

— ✱ —

A festival is a time of sacred ritual. Through symbolic dramas, consecrations, sacrifices, music, dances, and contests, a festival recreates mythic history, enacts the worldview of the culture, observes the great round of life and death, and revitalizes both individual and community by reconnecting them with the numinous. The festival is mythically significant for its celebration of sacred stories, which re-create the world with each retelling. It is phantasmagorical as it plays with the very shapes of reality, bending gender, turning social mores upside down, offering up one's suffering to the gods in hopes of bringing the world back to life. It is transcendent in its vision of possibilities that otherwise go unexperienced and unbelieved. Its beauty is in the way it reenchants the world on a regular basis.

As we learned earlier from Johan Huizinga in *Homo Ludens,* the instinct to feast and the instinct to play are intimately connected, the link between them being the desire to celebrate. The idea of playing in the sacred sphere of the gods, Huizinga points out, goes back to Plato. The entire universe, Plato believed, is permeated by the play-spirit and is on display for all to see at the festival; religion itself is a form of sacred play in honor of the deity. Some argue that play pales in comparison with religion because it is less serious. However, Huizinga writes, "The Platonic identification of play and holiness does not defile the latter by calling it play, rather it exalts the concept of play to the highest regions of the spirit . . . In play we may move below the level of the serious, as the child does; but we can also move above it—in the realm of the beautiful and the sacred."

For the Greeks of antiquity, life was a *play*—and was *to be played* if one was to find an answer to the question of one's fate or destiny. "Coupled with this play-sense," writes Huizinga, "is a spirit that strives for honor, dignity, superiority and beauty. Magic and mystery, heroic longings, the foreshadowings of music, sculpture and logic all seek form and expression in noble play."

In this light Joseph Campbell writes in *The Masks of God:*

From the position of secular man (Homo sapiens), that is to say, we are to enter the play sphere of the festival, acquiescing in a game of belief, where fun, joy, and rapture rule in ascending series. The laws of life in time and space—economics, politics, and even morality—will thereupon dissolve. Whereafter, re-created by that return to paradise before the Fall, before the knowledge of good and evil, right and wrong, true and false, belief and disbelief, we are to carry the point of view and spirit of man the player (Homo ludens) back into life; as in the play of children, where, undaunted by the banal actualities of life's meager possibilities, the spontaneous impulse of the spirit to identify itself with something other than itself for the sheer delight of play transubstantiates the world—in which, actually, after all, things are not quite as real or permanent, terrible, important, or logical as they seem.

Throughout human history, Campbell emphasizes, the festival's purpose has been to transfigure the unbearably harsh realities of life into bearable realities, and it has done so by lifting the spirit of the individual and the group through ecstatic rituals and through the trials of competition and contest.

Reflecting its intense devotion to the gods and to a world-view that saw the universe as sacred and worthy of constant celebration, ancient Greece abounded in festivals. Prominent among them were the Great Mysteries held at Eleusis, celebrating Demeter and Persephone; seven different Dionysian festivals, which combined religious celebrations honoring the god of the vine with dramatic contests; and the Panathenaia gatherings in Athens, a thanksgiving festival for the glory of Athena that featured competitions in music, poetry, and athletics.

Far less recognized or studied is the sheer proliferation of athletic festivals across the country. In the early classical era, the sixth century B.C.E., most towns honored their gods by staging simple local games. By 500 B.C.E., there were at least fifty regularly scheduled games, three hundred by the first century C.E.

By the middle of the fifth century B.C.E., there were stadiums in every large city, plus gymnasiums and *palaistras*, or wrestling schools, in most towns. These enormously popular spaces served as social clubs but also as training grounds for both body and soul. The fabled "gilded youth" regarded the gymnasiums as second homes where they exercised daily and competed in games. Aristocratic and educated men also visited them daily for physical and intellectual exercise—a friendly wrestling match or a good conversation. Philosophers, orators, and historians were especially fond of them as places where they were allowed to lecture. In his never-ending search for good conversation, Socrates visited the *agora*, or marketplace, but also an outdoor gymnasium, situated in a beautiful olive grove just outside Athens, called the Academy. After Plato established his philosophical school there, those who studied with him were called Academics.

The Academy is the setting for one of Plato's most famous *Dialogues*, "Laches," an account of Socrates' discussing the virtues of athletic training and the nature of courage with two generals. When they get caught up in insignificant details, such as armor and bridles, Socrates reminds them that learning to fight in armor is "only a means to an end." The real purpose is to strengthen something far deeper. "It is the self, the soul, of the young men that this training is going to be applied to," says Socrates. "But which of us knows what is good for the soul, that is the real question."

"The sixth century saw the peak of the splendor and popularity of athletics in Greece," writes Will Durant in *The Story of Civilization*. "In 582 [B.C.E]. the Amphiphictyonic League established the Pythian games in honor of Apollo at Delphi; in the same year the Isthmian games were instituted at Corinth in honor of Poseidon; six years later the Nemean games were inaugurated to celebrate the Nemean Zeus; and all three occasions became Panhellenic festivals. Together with the Olympic games they formed a *periodis* or cycle and the great ambition of a Greek athlete was to win the crown in all of them."

As their political and cultural influence spread, the Greeks became known across the Mediterranean for their philosophers, artists, sculptors, and scientists, but also for their illustrious runners, wrestlers, and chariot drivers. The increase in athletic festivals and the esteem in which they were held gave them an importance among the Greeks unrivaled in any culture in history. "At the close of the sixth century," writes E. Norman Gardiner, "the Greeks were literally a nation of athletes."

It was this fledgling nation of spirited athletes and philosopher-coaches that responded enthusiastically every four years when word went out across the Greek empire that it was time to gather at distant Olympia for the Festival of Zeus. Nothing could have pleased the Greek politicians more than this massive gathering of athletes and spectators, which strengthened the bonds of national identity as citizens of the hundred-plus city-states came together in peaceful interaction.

While politics, religion, art, and language did not unite the Greeks in the way they dreamed about and schemed after, Durant concludes, their athletic festivals nearly did. And one of the most effective instruments in forging this sense of common identity and mutual respect was the short-lived but consistent period of peace that accompanied each Olympiad.

CALLING THE TRUCE

One of the most sacred objects in all of Greek antiquity was an inscribed discus stored in the temple of Hera at Olympia. It was removed only once every four years, a month before the Olympic Games began, when the high priests presented it to the *spondophoroi*, the official truce heralds. With the discus in hand they set forth across the far-flung empire to announce the *ekecheira*, the sacred truce.

Miraculously, a contemporary description survives. "The Olympic Truce is written on a discus," writes Pausanius. "The writing is not in a straight line, but in a circle around the edge of the discus." He describes it as the "the discus of Iphitos," a

The Truce Discus was carried across ancient Greece to announce the upcoming Games at Olympia and to declare the cessation of all hostilities for the Games' duration.

reference to the king of Elis who had revived the Games and forged the truce, and as being "made of gold and ivory, and created by a certain Kolotes of Herakleia or Paros."

The heralds wore olive wreaths and carried special staffs that declared their inviolate status to soldiers or travelers of dubious character they might meet along the road. Thus protected, they traveled to each city-state to proclaim the date of the Games (which, according to Gardiner, coincided with the second or third full moon after the summer solstice) and invite the local Greek-speaking male citizens to compete for the laurels. Those prospective pilgrims who hesitated to travel great distances in hostile times were reminded by the heralds of the truce's terms, first declared by Apollo in the inspired voice of the Delphic oracle herself. The three-month-long agreement demanded safe passage for the spectators, athletes, and trainers traveling to the Peloponnese. Ideally, wars were suspended, robberies curtailed. Anyone, whether soldier or peasant, who broke the truce was heavily fined. Wars raged throughout Greek history, but hostilities were halted often enough during the festivals, and personal antagonisms were ignored at the Olympic site effectively enough to give rise to the mythic belief that war itself had been banned.

For a month after the trumpeted announcements, the rough-hewn roads of Greece teemed with tens of thousands of pilgrims, merchants, politicians, ambassadors, and athletes—including Athenians, Spartans, Dorians, Ionians, Macedonians, and Ephesians—traveling on horseback, in carts and chariots, and on foot to Olympia. So effective was the truce that Socrates chided a fearful friend, "But why do you fear the journey? Don't you walk around nearly all day at home? Don't you walk to lunch? And again to have dinner? And to have sleep? Don't you see that if you string together all the walking you do in five or six days anyway you could easily travel from Athens to Olympia?"

The spirit that moved through the festival came from the belief that if the finest young men of Greece came together in peaceful but passionate competition while watched by the multitudes, then a sense of national unity might be inspired. Lysias of Syracuse, in his *Olympic Oration*, recommended that his fellow Greeks make the pilgrimage to the festival, saying that if they witnessed the contests in which "men matched their strength and their wealth and to hear the dissertations of the philosophers it would plant the seed of friendship in their hearts."

Considering the brutal warfare of the time, waged both by and against Greece, the notion of a three-month period of peace every four years was a monumental achievement. In the nineteenth century, philosopher William James called for a "substitute for war's disciplinary function . . . a moral equivalent of war." The ancient Olympic truce was just such an evolutionary vision of how human beings can sublimate their martial instincts. While only a rarely reached ideal, the truce seized the imagination of the world and has not let go.

THE PAGEANTRY AND THE PANORAMA

The simple sacred grove at Olympia, dotted with dozens of ashen altars, eventually evolved into a stunning sanctuary "adorned with temples, treasuries, halls, and statues," according to Pausanius, when he visited in the second century C.E. He counted sixteen *zanes*, or bronze statues of Zeus, erected by athletes caught cheating in their events and inscribed with stern reminders about the moral code expected at the Olympics. One such inscription reads: "You win with the speed of your feet and the strength in your body, and not with money!" Other visitors through the centuries remarked on the splendor of the art, left behind by diplomats hoping to curry favor with the gods, making Olympia a kind of open-air museum.

Brooding over the entire sanctuary was the temple of Zeus. Within its chambers was the awe-inspiring statue by Phidias, named by Herodotus as one of the Seven Wonders of the Ancient World. The Roman orator Cicero wrote that Phidias "had a vision of beauty in his mind so perfect that concentrating on it he could direct his artist's hand to produce a real likeness of the god." The inspired vision produced a colossal figure of the ruler of Olympia constructed out of ivory, gold, and chryselephantine. The thirty-three-foot-high statue sat on a throne of ebony and ivory, flanked by two recumbent lions made of solid gold. In one hand, Zeus held a scepter "of every imaginable metal" and, in the other hand, a six-foot winged ivory-and-gold figure of Nike, or Victory, signifying triumph in the Games. Around his head, according to Pausanius, was "a sculpted wreath of olive sprays," a visual reference to the simple reward for each champion during the Games.

"No other statue was so admired by the Greeks," writes Roberto Calasso, "nor even by Zeus himself, who hurled an approving thunderbolt down on the black paving when Phidias finished the job and asked the god for a sign."

When the weary but exhilarated travelers arrived at Olympia, they encountered a festival like none other. Religion, the arts, philosophy, politics, and sport stood shoulder to shoulder, like the travelers themselves. The exciting spectacle mirrored the nation's zest for life, a hallmark of the Greek genius from Socrates to Zorba.

The Olympic festival stood out as in bas-relief from all the others, E. Norman Gardiner writes, because it was "the national religious festival of the whole Greek race. Olympia was the meeting place of the Greek world." To imagine this charged atmosphere at its height, in the mid-fifth century, we must try to envision a montage of the World Series at Yankee Stadium (or the World Cup at Wembley Stadium), a United Nations conference, an art exhibition worthy of the Louvre, and a music competition as rigorous as that of Salzburg, all being held during Christmas Week in Jerusalem—with a Burning Man–style all-night revelry after each day's competitions. In *The Story of Civilization*, Durant beautifully describes the cosmic carnival atmosphere:

> It was a fair as well as a festival. The plain was covered not only with the tents that sheltered the visitors from the July heat, but with booths where a thousand concessionaires exposed for sale everything from wine and fruit to horses and statuary, while acrobats and conjurors performed their tricks for the crowd. Some juggled balls in the air, others performed marvels of agility and skill, others ate fire or swallowed swords: modes of amusement, like forms of superstition, enjoy a reverend antiquity. Famous orators like Gorgias, famous sophists like Hippias, perhaps famous writers like Herodotus, delivered addresses or recitations from the porticoes of the Temple of Zeus.

ON THE THRESHOLD

The ten officials, or *hellanodikai*, "judges of the Greeks," in Elis were required to begin planning the festivities ten months ahead of the opening ceremonies. They organized the cleaning of the site, the repair of the statues, the arrangement of the events. During the same ten-month period, prospective athletes were expected to be in training, the last month being compulsory training under the eye of the officials at Elis. The athletes arrived with a spartan equipment bag. No shoes, no shorts; only a jar of olive oil as sun protection and a *strigil*, a curved blade for scraping off the oil at the end of the day. Their training was organized by the officials and held in the local gymnasium, *palaistra*, and practice track. The practice drills were enforced by the *paidotribai*, the infamous whip-wielding trainers. The athletes were indeed "whipped into shape" by the regimen, strict diet, and elite standards for qualifying for the Games.

The first-century philosopher Epictetus, one of history's great chroniclers of the well-lived life and a great fan of the Olympics, colorfully described the demands on contemporary athletes: "You say, 'I want to win at Olympia'... If you do, you will have to obey instructions, eat according to regulations, keep away from desserts, exercise on a fixed schedule, in both heat and cold; you must not drink cold water nor can you have a drink of wine whenever you want. You must hand yourself over to a coach as you would a doctor. Then in the contest itself you must gouge and be gouged, there will be times when you will sprain a wrist, turn your ankle, swallow mouthfuls of sand, and be flogged. And after all that there are times when you lose."

During this period the Olympic officials checked each athlete's credentials, especially whether or not he was of bona fide Greek descent—for only true Greeks could compete on the sacred grounds of Zeus's own sanctuary. Barbarians (those who couldn't speak Greek) were allowed to watch but not compete. The athletes were closely scrutinized. The unqualified were disqualified; only the best of the best were allowed to perform for the glory of Zeus. "If you have worked so as to be worthy of going to Olympia," the officials told the athletes, "if you have done nothing indolent nor ignoble, take heart and march on; but those who have not so trained may leave and go wherever they like."

Two days before the festival, the procession of judges, priests, and competitors—the last often accompanied by their fathers, brothers, and personal trainers—with horses and chariots in full regalia, set out from Elis and traveled along the Sacred Way to Olympia, a distance of about fifty-eight kilometers. Along the route, the priests might stop the procession's progress to sacrifice a pig or perform other rites that reminded everyone of the Games' ultimate purpose, the honoring of Zeus.

Each day of the ancient Games was the equivalent of an act in a long theatrical play—the posing and resolving of the dramatic question: what is worthy of memory, emulation, and enactment? Here, in an atmosphere of sacred festival, spiritual preparation, and respect for fair competition as the ultimate arbiter of an athlete's worthiness, we find the roots of our own profound responses to what Pindar called "the splendid contests." Being grounded in prayer, sacrifice, vows, and thanksgiving, the Games began, unfolded, and ended in ritual. The contests were held as an offering to the gods, in honor of one's family and city, in a spirit of heroism. Poet and naturalist writer Annie Dillard captured the beauty of the sacred approach in her book, *Holy the Firm*: "Every day is a god, each day is a god, and I worship each god. I praise each day splintered down, and wrapped in time like a husk, a husk of many colors spreading, all dawn fast over the mountains split."

These words could have been those of a pilgrim waking up at Olympia on the first day of the festival.

THE FIRST DAY

The first day inaugurated the festival with ceremonies, rituals, contests for heralds and trumpeters, and contests for boys. The morning, began with the athletes and their trainers, fathers, brothers, and uncles walking together in a ceremonial procession to the *Bouleuterion*, or Council Building, where the Olympic archives were kept, to swear the Olympic oath. Underscoring the competition's dedication to the glory of Zeus, the athletes stood before a statue of Zeus Horkios, Enforcer of Oaths, who held a thunderbolt in each hand—an image that struck terror in the hearts of all who saw it, Pausanius says. The athletes were again severely scrutinized by the ten judges, who wore the royal color purple in honor of King Iphitus. Then they were sworn to the oath over the entrails of a sacrificed animal. "It is established for the athletes," Pausanius writes, "their fathers and brothers, and their trainers to swear an oath on slices of the flesh of wild boars that they will do nothing evil against the Olympic Games. The athletes . . . also swear in addition that they have adhered strictly to their training for ten successive months."

Pausanius adds that the judges took their own solemn oath that they would "judge fairly and without taking bribes, and [that] they will guard in secrecy everything about the examinee." They were noted for their impartiality and their honest verdicts. In accordance with tradition, the meat, having been blessed, was not eaten. As Francis Huxley writes, ritual sacrifice is "the death that gives life." A sacrifice is literally an act that "makes sacred." In the case of the athletic festival, it sanctified the contests that followed. Without the sacrifices, the Greeks believed, the festival would have been not sacred but profane—that which is outside of or other than sacred.

After the swearing-in ceremony, the athlete was free to wander around the Altis, the sacred precinct, and admire the many altars, such as those in honor of Hera, Hestia, and Gaia and the major one dedicated to Zeus. Depending on his confidence about the upcoming competitions, a competitor might sacrifice an animal and offer it up to his patron god or hero, whether Zeus, Hermes, Apollo, Herakles, or even Pelops, or seek out a priest to examine the entrails for an omen of victory. Gardiner writes: "Throughout the day there were many other sacrifices and rites both public and private of which we know nothing. Competitors would offer their vows at the altars of the various gods or heroes whom they regarded as their patrons. Others would go off to the stadium for a final practice. The crowd of sightseers would wander round the *altis*, following in the train of some celebrity, athletic or otherwise, admiring the sculptures of the new temple, or listening to some rhapsodist reciting Homer, some poet reading his verses, some orator displaying his eloquence or sophistries."

While meandering around the sanctuary an athlete might also visit the Herarion, where the discus was kept, as a player today might visit a Hall of Fame. Or he might wander over to the Temple of Zeus to admire the sculptures commemorating the twelve labors of Herakles placed in the metopes high above the columns, much as an All-Star ballplayer today might marvel at the championship banners high in the rafters at Boston Garden or the plaques with the names of former Yankee greats in Yankee Stadium's deep centerfield.

But beyond the ritual atmosphere, the splendor of the temples, and the romance of the stadium, gymnasium, and hippodrome, the experience was an ordeal for most of the athletes and spectators. "The Olympic Games are pretty uncomfortable," writes Epictetus. "You are scorched by the sun and crushed by the crowd. There are no decent toilets. You get soaked when it rains and you are deafened by the constant noise. But it's all worth it for the brilliant events you see."

The afternoon of the first day was dedicated to three events—running, wrestling, and boxing competitions for boys, who were defined as being under age sixteen.

The champion of the boys' wrestling competitions at the sixtieth Olympiad in 540 B.C.E. was Milo of Croton (now in southern Italy), who went on to win men's wrestling titles in six straight Olympiads, the last in 516, when he was in his forties.

He also won several wrestling titles at the Pythian, Isthmian, and Nemean Games. Legends of his strength abound. The ancient writers say that he trained for the Games by carrying a calf every day until it grew into a bull. But it wasn't just his strength that was admired, it was his *control* of that power. This self-control was celebrated in numerous legends, such as how he could hold a pomegranate in his fist so tightly that no could take it away— yet so lightly that not a drop of juice fell to the ground. He was also known for his ability to balance on an iron disk greased with olive oil—and defeat anyone who dared try to push him off.

His identification with the mythical Herakles, whose task was also controlling his immense strength, is implicit in all the stories associated with Milo, including his wearing a lion's skin and carrying a club into battle. He was renowned for putting fellow soldiers and friends ahead of him, as in the story of his single-handedly holding up the roof of a collapsing hall until everyone escaped, and only then saving his own hide.

Today we honor athletes in ways that reflect the values of our time. Similarly, the ancient Greeks recorded hundreds of stories that embodied their ideals, such as Milo's legendary harmony of body and mind, strength and courage. These accounts, as they traveled down through the centuries, have carried the spirit of the ancient Games to us—an ideal spirit endorsed in the words of the late, great sportswriter/philosopher Red Smith: "People who brag about telling it like it is would do the world a favor by telling it like it should be."

THE SECOND DAY

For most pilgrims and athletes, the Games didn't really begin until the early morning of the second day. That was when the immensely popular chariot and horse races were staged at the

ORIGINS OF
THE ANCIENT OLYMPIC EVENTS

Event	Date (B.C.E.)	City of Victor
200-meter race	776	Elis
400-meter race	724	Elis
4,800-meter race	720	Sparta
pentathlon	708	Sparta
wrestling	708	Sparta
boxing	688	Smyrna
chariot race	680	Thebes
horse race	648	Crannon (Thessaly)
pankration	648	Syracuse
boys' 200-meters	632	Elis
boys' wrestling	632	Sparta
boys' boxing	616	Sybaris (now S. Italy)
race in armor	520	Heraea (Arcadia)

Here we see the origin date for each of the ancient Olympic events and the city or district from which the champion hailed that year. The table thus illustrates the slow evolution of the program and how long the program remained intact, until the dissolution of the Games in 393 C.E. Source: Michael L. Finley and H. W. Pleket, The Olympic Games.

hippodrome, a rectangular 600-yard-long course laid out in front of a high embankment where the spectators sat. The spectacle began with an official procession that entered the hippodrome, led by the judges, dressed in garlands and royal robes; the herald and the trumpeter; and the two-wheeled chariots, each drawn by four horses, that would compete in the first race.

When all were ready, the herald proclaimed each competitor's name, his father's name, and his city, and asked if any man had any charges to bring against him. If there were no claims against any athletes, the Games were declared open.

The chariots lined up at the long, staggered starting gate and waited for the signal to be given by an elaborate mechanism featuring a bronze dolphin that descended onto the gate, triggering a bronze eagle to "fly." According to Pausanius, "From then on, it is all a matter of the skill of the drivers and the speed of the horses."

In his play *Electra*, Sophocles has left us a breathtaking description of Orestes' tragedy in a chariot race at the Pythian Games:

> They stood by while the judges cast the lots, and arranged the order of the chariots. Then, at the brazen trumpet blast, they were off. All shook their reins and urged their horses on with shouts. The whole track was filled with the noise of rattling cars [chariots] and the dust rose to heaven. All were bunched together and none spared the whip as each tried to break out of the pack and leave behind the whirling wheels and snorting steeds, for each saw his wheels splattered with foam and felt the breath of horses on his back. Orestes as he turned the farther stele [pillar] held close and grazed it with the hub of his wheel, giving rein to his right horse but pulling in the nearer one. For a time all were safe and sound, but at the turn between the sixth and seventh lap . . . one

after another fell into [a] single crash and smashed up and the whole Kriaisian plain was filled with wreckage.

As the closing ritual act of the chariot race, the herald announced the name of the victor, followed by his father's name and the city from which he hailed. Only the richest Greeks could afford horses, and it was the owner of the winning chariot who was awarded the crown of olive leaves taken from the sacred wild olive near the Temple of Zeus. But the owners were rarely trained to compete in chariot races, so they would have slaves, soldiers, and even women drive their chariots. This is why reports survive of ordinary citizens, slaves, and women—essentially drivers-for-hire—competing and sometimes emerging victorious, their glory later extolled in song and in stone inscriptions. The daughter of King Archidamos of Sparta, Kyniska, was the victor in the four-horse chariot race at two consecutive Olympiads, in 396 and 392 B.C.E.

After the chariot race came the horse race, a single lap of six stades, or 1,200 yards. It was deliriously dangerous. The jockeys rode without shoes or stirrups, and the chronicles reveal that many riders fell and were maimed or killed.

Early in the sixth century, the pentathlon—a set of five events—was added to the program for the second day. "When King Iphitos restored the games, the people had forgotten the ancient customs," writes Pausanius. "Gradually they did remember and so new events were added to the Games . . . At the 18th Olympiad, they remembered the pentathlon and wrestling." The pentathlon's first four events—discus, long jump, javelin, and wrestling—took place in front of the Altar of Zeus. The fifth, the *stade*, or sprint-race, was held in the stadium.

In a tone of awe that presages our own respect for modern decathlon champions, the Eighth Ode of Bacchylides describes Automedes of Phlius, winner of the pentathlon at the Nemean Games: "He shone among the other pentathletes as the bright moon in the middle of the month dims the radiance of the stars; even thus he showed his lovely body to the great ring of watching Greeks, as he threw the round discus and hurled the shaft of black-leaved alder from his grasp to the steep heights of heaven, and roused the cheers of the spectators by his lithe movements in the wrestling at the end."

At the ancient Games there was no high jump competition, only the long jump. From vase paintings and the chronicles of ancient observers we know that competitors held jumping weights made of lead, called *halteres*, and swung them so they could leap farther. Although records from the ancient contests are almost nonexistent, there is an inscription about a much-honored naval commander, Phayllus of Croton, that reads: "He jumped five over fifty feet, but threw the discus five short of a hundred." Considering that the modern long jump record, held by American Mike Powell, is 29 feet, 4½ inches, scholars believe that the ancient writers were describing something resembling our own triple jump. But the fame of Phayllus lies elsewhere, anyway. The reason he never won at Olympia was because he ventured there in 482 B.C.E., just as the Persians were approaching Salamis. He contributed his ship to the defense of Greece and thus never reached Olympia. His actions were immortalized by Aristophanes and by Alexander the Great, ensuring that his tale of self-sacrifice for the glory of Greece would live on.

At the end of the second day, the crowds assembled at the Pelopeion, the shrine of the hero Pelops, and paid him tribute with the sacrifice of a black ram. The victors of the day's events were honored in the sanctuary; thereafter followed a second night of revelry.

THE THIRD DAY

A race is a contest between two or more individuals, but it is also a metaphor for the distance in life that we travel. The sight of a simple footrace, whether run by children or Olympic champions, provides the simplest of pleasures, the most elemental of thrills. Homer captures the universal desire to run like the wind in the *Odyssey* when he has the wily Odysseus ask of Athena, "O, goddess, hear me, and come and put more speed in my feet." Twenty-eight centuries later, at the 1984 Los Angeles Olympic Games, Japanese filmmaker Kon Ichikawa created a short film about sprinters called *The Fastest*. The narrator's voice comments, "The one hundred meters [race] represents modern human existence . . . Modern man's mechanized thirst for freedom changes ten seconds into an eternity."

Something of this spirit is compacted into the laconic description of the winner in the very first Olympiad, in 776 B.C.E. The victors' list says simply, "Kourebos, the cook, won the footrace." In the first thirteen Olympiads the *stade*, a short sprint-race of about 192 meters down the length of the stadium, was the only event. Even after longer races were added to the Olympic program, the short sprint remained the most venerable of all the contests.

According to E. Norman Gardiner, the third and central day of the festival was scheduled to fall on the full moon, possibly an echo of older fertility rites. This was the day the Greeks "started from scratch." This ancient expression has its origins in the footraces of the earliest Olympics, which began with the runners standing behind a scratch or mark in the sand. The old saying also highlights what Ludwig Drees calls "the original basis of the festival," the sprint-race and the sacrifice to Zeus.

The third day began with a grand religious celebration, a high point of the festival, marked by a solemn procession of ambassadors carrying gifts of gold and silver, prayers of gratitude being offered to the gods, and the great sacrifice of a hundred bulls at the Altar of Zeus. In the afternoon, with the ambience of gift-giving, sacrifice, and praise still palpable, three footraces were staged. Honoring the third day's heightened sacrality, on that day alone each race finished at the western end of the stadium with the runners facing the sacred Altis, a reminder of the ultimate purpose of their running—the honor of Zeus.

The first of the footraces, the *dolikhos*, was also the longest—twenty-four lengths of the running track, or 4,600 meters (2¼ miles). This was followed by the *diaulos*, the middle-distance race, run at two lengths of the stadium, comparable to the modern 400-meter race.

The third race, the short sprint, was the most beloved of all the contests at Olympia, not only for its venerability but also because of its association with Herakles and his brothers. Each Olympiad was named after the winner of this race, which offered a convenient way to establish one chronology for all of Greece at a time when each city-state used a separate calendar. The classical writer Statius has rendered an invaluable description of sprinters running in place, beating their chests to get the blood moving, practicing short, quick sprints. Eventually, a *balbis*, or stone sill, replaced the simple scratch in the sand. Thereafter, the contest began when the runners received permission to wedge their toes into the grooves of the stone sills and were reminded to listen for the signal to start the race—either the herald's trumpet blast or the shout: *Apite!* Go! Overly eager runners who were guilty of false starts were punished with a few lashes of the officials' whip.

One of the greatest honors in ancient Olympic history was the title "Triastes," conferred upon an athlete who won the *stade*, the *diaulos*, and the *dolichos* in the same year. This astonishing feat would be roughly the equivalent of a single athlete— a protean, shape-shifting combination of Paavo Nurmi, Michael

Johnson, and Jesse Owens—winning the 5,000-meters, 400-meters, and 100-meters in the same Olympiad today. And yet this was accomplished—in four consecutive Olympiads, from 164 to 152 B.C.E.—by the immortal Leonidas of Rhodes, described by Pausanius as "twelve times conqueror through his swiftness of foot."

The third day of the Olympic festival closed with a ritual banquet supplied by the day's sacrifice.

THE FOURTH DAY

The fourth was the fighting day, highlighted by wrestling, boxing, and the *pankration,* all of which were held in front of the Great Altar. The spectators yelled the names of their favorite athletes and cheered for them as raucously as fans at a modern boxing or wrestling match. By contemporary consensus, the toughest of all ancient events was boxing. With its roots in literal duels to the death during ritual funeral games, it was a deadly serious affair throughout Olympic history. The images of boxers that have survived in Greek sculptures, paintings, and literary descriptions give us some idea of how disfigured these athletes were after years of relentless pounding. The rules of the time were practically no rules at all: no fixed rounds, no limits on technique except for holding and gouging. A self-effacing boxer named Androleus immortalized himself and his fiercely combative world with these ringing words: "Now Pisa has one of Androleus' ears and Plataea one of his eyes; in Pytho they thought I was dead." Fights could and often did last for hours, until one of the boxers was knocked unconscious, gave in, or perhaps was killed—which was considered less disgraceful than giving up.

The acme of accomplishment in boxing was to win without taking a single blow from your rival, but Dio Chrystostom records a story that goes even further—that of the undefeated Melankomas of Caria, victor in 49 C.E., at the 207th Olympiad. Melankomas never delivered a punch nor took one. He combined the wit and wiles of Odysseus with the tactics and technique of the young Muhammad Ali as he wore down his opponents through constant evasion, exasperating them with his endurance. Chrystostom believed Melankomas's approach to boxing was artistic and philosophical; Melankomas did not want to force the decision, nor did he wish to be passive and let himself be hurt. Instead, he cultivated an early Greek version of judo, in which yielding to the spirit of the moment is considered strength and gentle determination outlasts brute force.

The *pankration* was literally an "all-strength," and figuratively a "no-holds-barred," contest. It combined boxing and wrestling and allowed the competitors to fight with their hands, feet, elbows, knees, and even their heads, which encouraged gouging, strangling, and choking. The goal was the complete submission and surrender of your opponent. The grislier aspects of the competition were overshadowed by what its proponents considered its radiant qualities. Ludwig Drees explains: "The athletes who entered for the pankration needed great strength of will; they were not allowed to show fear." Its most admired champion was Theagenes of Thasos. "His ambition was, I think, to rival Achilles," writes Pausanius, "by winning a prize for running in the fatherland of the swiftest of those who are called heroes. The total number of crowns that he won was one thousand four hundred."

Of all the contests in the Games, the one that best evokes martial origins would have to be the *hoplitodromos*, the race in armor. Watching athletes wearing metal helmets and brandishing bronze shields as they raced two lengths of the stadium—

nearly four hundred meters—under the brunt of the afternoon sun must have been a harsh reminder of athletics' original purpose—preparation for battle. Pausanius even claims that the event was first held, in 520 B.C.E., at the 65th Olympiad, under the guise of a military exercise.

THE FIFTH DAY: HAIL TO THE VICTOR VALIANT

An old Greek saying has it, "If a man is good, he is happy; if he is happy, he is good." In the rarified atmosphere of the ancient Olympics the victors were good men and very happy men, and they were celebrated accordingly. Thus the last day of the festival was spent in feasting and rejoicing.

The winners were led in procession past the ancient wild olive tree sacred to Zeus, where, following ancient tradition, a boy whose parents were still alive cut a leafy branch from an olive tree using a golden sickle. The leaves were woven into crown wreaths and in front of the statue of Zeus bestowed upon the champions, who gave thanks to the god and were then heralded by having their names proclaimed to the great gathering. Finally, each victor was handed a palm frond, an ancient symbol of victory. When all the victors had been crowned, their fathers, brothers, friends, and guests rushed forward to congratulate them, and excited spectators threw handfuls of leaves and flower petals into the air.

"Here under the rubric of athletics," Durant writes, "we find the real religion of the Greeks—the worship of health, beauty, and strength." Today, when commentators refer to sports as our "religion," they are not elucidating a uniquely modern phenomenon as much as they are harkening back to the very roots of Western civilization. In ancient Greece, sport was one of many revered ways to create community over and over again. In much the same way, our modern culture of sports is a passionately felt communal experience, one of the few that allow us to sense our shared values, common emotions, and collective dreams.

THE OLYMPIC WOMEN

One of the oldest founding stories of the Olympic sanctuary, the divine marriage of King Pelops and Queen Hippodameia, includes a gendered symmetry unusual for ancient Greece. While the Olympic Games were established by Pelops in thanks to Zeus for his victory over King Oinomaos, Hippodameia initiated the women's games, the Heraea, in honor of Hera, Zeus's wife.

According to classics professor Thomas F. Scanlon, the women's festival was held during the period just before each Olympiad. The central event was a set of three footraces for girls organized by the leading women of nearby Elis. There are only three surviving accounts to give us an idea of the role of women in Greek athletics, the most substantial one being Pausanius's description of the Heraea: "The contest is a race for maidens of various ages: in the first race are the youngest, and next those slightly older, and last of all the eldest. They all run with their hair down their back, a short tunic reaching just below the knees and their right shoulder bare to the breast. They use . . . the regular racecourse at Olympia but make it a sixth part of a stade [about 160 meters or 173 yards] shorter. And the victors receive crowns of olive and part of the heifer sacrificed to Hera."

The Heraea winners were allowed the honor of immortalizing their Olympic victory with a work of art. But rather than erecting statues, as the male winners did, the women commissioned paintings of themselves, which were hung in the colonnade of Hera's temple, close to the spot where the Olympic torch is lit today.

Women sprinters racing at the Heraea, or Women's Olympics.
Greek redware pottery, late 6th century B.C.E.

The strict rules against women's participation in the main Olympic competition, and the strictures against their even watching the Games, are part of the larger problem of women's place in Greek society. Richard Woff, lecturer at the University of London, attributes the exclusion to the close association between athletics and war. "As it was men who did the fighting, athletics were also closely connected with the whole idea of being and becoming a man. For this reason, there was usually no place for women in ancient Greek athletics."

There were lively exceptions, however, which we know about because of evidence on "one stone alone," to cite the haunting phrase of H. A. Harris, avid sportsman and professor of classics at St. David's College in Wales. A single inscription from Delphi proudly describes the victories of three sisters who won running and chariot races at women's athletic meetings in Delphi, Nemea, Sicyon, and Epidaurus. Beyond this single shred of stone evidence, we have only Plato's recommendations, in the *Republic*, that women should receive athletic training in the ideal state, plus historical writings that tell us of Spartan women being encouraged to train vigorously in athletics. There are also a few scattered reports of girls wrestling with boys on the island of Chios and in what is now Italy, as recorded by Suetonius and Juvenal. Beyond these, there is only a long silence about opportunities for women in the sporting life of the classical world.

THE DECLINE AND FALL

Ironically, it was around the middle of the fifth century B.C.E., during the so-called Golden Age of Greece, that the character of the Games began their slow decline. The paradox may be partly attributed to the increasing wealth, prosperity, and power of Greece, causing a corresponding increase in professionalism in the Games. Another often-cited reason is the fading of religious fervor, suggesting that the Games had retained their vitality as long as they had a higher, spiritual purpose—the honor of Zeus. Other factors included a shift of focus from the athletes to the spectators and an overemphasis on prizes and the rewards that awaited the athletes at home, which in due time led to all kinds of chicanery, such as bribing trainers and officials. Later commentators, such as Epicurus and the physician Galen— not unlike some intellectuals today who feel overshadowed by the cult of celebrity athletes—complained about the attention showered upon the Games.

After the Olympic festival was banned in 393 and the temples were razed in the following years, a series of earthquakes (in 522 and 551) and floods buried the site under twelve feet of mud. The sanctuary was hidden and nearly forgotten for the next twelve hundred years. Yet the echoes of the ancient Games were still heard, not unlike the cries of the goddess Echo, left behind when the other gods fled the coming of the new god and the new religion. Her cries can still be discerned by those who have learned to listen. Similarly, the Olympic spirit lived on, preserved in chronicles and on pots, vases, and murals, interwoven into classical poetry, philosophy, and drama. The echoes were heard by Renaissance scholars who translated the classical authors and by eighteenth-century German archaeologists who dug among the mute stones of Athens, Olympia, Delphi, and other sites. Those translations, and the stories of those discoveries, came to the attention of Soutsos in Greece, Brookes in England, and Coubertin in France.

Much as the young Pericles had admonished the citizens of Athens for their "inferiority to the Spartans in physical excellence," these three men chided their fellow citizens for their lack of fitness, then offered up the vision of a revival of athletic competition so modern men and women, too, might regain their honor, dignity, health, and spirit. Their overlapping roles in reviving the spirit of the ancient Olympics are evocative of the story told by Pindar about Alkimedon of Algina, wrestling champion at the Games of 460 B.C.E., who "breathed new life into the nostrils of his aged grandfather."

Likewise, these three visionaries sought to breathe new life into the aged Games and rekindle the sacred flame that had burned for so long at Olympia. In so doing, they helped revive the myth of sports, the collective dream that noble forms of play—serious play—can renew the body, mind, and soul. Their efforts also revived our ancient capacity to experience what Michael Murphy calls "the essential ecstasy of sports." We have been "beside ourselves"—the original meaning of *ecstasy*—with conflicting emotions of pride and pain, love and sorrow, ever since, as the Olympic festivals dramatize for us the universal dream of overcoming life's greatest struggles with courage and determination.

THE STRUGGLE
FOR REVIVAL AND
THE PASSING OF
THE TORCH

—————————— ❋ ——————————

1896–1980

The important thing in the Olympic Games is
not to win but to take part;
the important thing in life is not the triumph
but the struggle.

—THE OLYMPIC CREED

As the ancient Greeks understood, great athletes
not only accept the ordeal of competition and the trial of
strength inherent in it, but also show us a connection
between what we do each day and something that is
larger than we are and lasts longer than we do.

— BILL BRADLEY, Olympian, 1964 Rome

— ✳ —

A certain mythic imagination suffused the ancient Games. All myths were regarded as sacred stories of how things came to be, and the ones that surrounded the Olympics elevated the festival's importance by connecting the place, the events, and the athletes with the sacred. The myths were reinforced by the Greek passion for rituals and ceremonies, which underscored their desire to please the gods with displays of religious piety, poetry, music, and dancing, as well as athletic prowess.

What humanist psychologist Rollo May calls "the cry for myth" is the longing in every generation for guiding stories, common "patterns of meaning," that hold us together as communities. May found, in his fifty years of work as a psychoanalyst, that the majority of myths are profoundly connected with "the passion to find our home." This is the core theme of the granddaddy of all myths, the Odyssey—the long and difficult journey to return to or even to *create* a home.

The myths that pervade the modern Olympics consist of stories, dreams, rituals, and images about the deeper dimensions of the sporting life, and they ultimately link us to the modern world's overarching story. The relationship between the ancient and modern myths of the Games is an intimate one; both respond to the holy longing for stories that connect us to the gods and to sacred space, and both provide us with collective meaning. In our own time, those stories tell of our feverish search for our roots, for the story that *roots* us. Sports in general—and the Olympics in particular—root us individually and collectively to a magical time and place. This is why they have been elevated to a place of mythic importance in the cultural imagination as one of our most powerful communal experiences and why sports have a grip on us that often feels irrational, tenacious, and ecstatic.

As mythologist Rebecca Armstrong told me in a recent interview, "Sports take us right into the heart of myth and ritual. Where else can we feel the exaltation of the human in its most defiant moment of temporal triumph—when the fragility and mortality of the human body is vanquished for those precious seconds and we see our fellow mortals shining with godly power? The oaths of honor, the parades, the uniforms, the medals, all parallel the warrior mythologies. These are the heroes who let us believe that the abyss between earth and heaven is not as far as it seems."

Since their revival in 1896, the Olympics have been surrounded by as many myths as there are dust devils under the feet of world-class sprinters. As we have seen, there has been considerable controversy over who gets credit for founding or reviving the modern Games, just as there were myriad stories contending for the distinction of official founding story of the ancient Games. Popular belief maintains that the modern Games were born out of the robust imagination of Baron de Coubertin, much as Athena burst forth out of the head of her father, Zeus. But as David C. Young discovered, the first revivals were actually staged decades earlier—in Greece in 1859, in London in 1866, and again in Athens in 1870. "The fact that they weren't international doesn't preclude them from being Olympics," he writes. "They had the spirit and name."

Then there is the much-maligned myth of amateurism, a nineteenth-century fantasy meant to remind modern athletes of the pure intentions of the ancient Greek athletes but really intended to keep the lower classes out of the Games, which many aristocrats felt were theirs alone. Young writes in *The Olympic Myth of Greek Amateur Athletics*, "Amateurism was strictly a modern concept born in England not much more than a century ago. It began as ideological means to justify an elitist athletic system that sought to bar the working class from competition. Most people nowadays think that amateurism was somehow the original state of our own organized sports, and that professional sports encroached on an earlier amateur system. The reverse is true."

The sudden explosion of competitive sports in the early nineteenth century, which occurred in England, Scotland, and in the United States, led to "professionalism." Wages and wagers followed glove-in-hand—or baseball glove in hand—echoing exactly the meaning of the ancient Greek word for athlete, *athlon*, "competitor for a prize." So exhilarating was the incursion of contests into everything from boxing to horse racing, rowing to running, that working-class athletes could make their living on tour, just as modern athletes do today. It also precipitated ferocious resistance from the newly formed amateur class, generally members of the landed gentry who were ferociously determined to compete only with those of their own class. Thus, the seed was planted for the mythologizing of the idea.

In 1931, Coubertin wrote in his *Olympic Memoirs* that he had "used a little deception," a romantic ruse, a nostalgic ploy, to get the attention he felt was needed to revive the ancient Games: "Amateurism, an admirable mummy that could transport to the museum . . . as a specimen of the modern art of embalming! A half a century has passed and it does not appear to have suffered from the constant manipulations of which it has been the object. It seems intact. Not one of us counted on such endurance . . . It provided me with a valuable screen to convene the Congress to Re-establish the Olympic Games. Seeing the importance which others lent it in the sporting world, I would show the expected zeal in that direction, but it was zeal without real conviction."

The phrase "admirable mummy" reflects Coubertin's understanding of the power of the myth of amateurism, which most believed was authentically ancient, noble, and Greek. Some would question it, but not enough to change it for fifty more years.

Another powerful mythic narrative at the heart of the Olympics is the perennial theme of paradise. Like King Iphitus before him, and Bart Giamatti, author of *Take Time for Paradise*, after him, Coubertin believed fairly contested games might help bring an age of global harmony. "Peace could be the product only of a better world," he wrote, "a better world could be brought about only by better individuals; and better individuals could be developed only by the give and take, the buffering and battering, the stress and strain of free competition." For Giamatti, all play, including organized and professional sports, "aspires to the condition of paradise." And what is paradise? It is the dream of a place outside of time and inside of sacred space where we are free again; this freedom is what is mirrored, "however fleetingly," in play or sport.

The Olympic Games' taking root early in the twentieth century meant that one of the most venerable plots from antiquity—the myth of sports—had returned to renew the times, and was in turn reshaped by them. Coubertin and the nascent Olympic movement proposed a mythic vision of athleticism and rationalism as positive influences on the world's youth. This vision was forced to compete, however, with the often nationalistic visions of proud countries fighting for the prestige and money that accompanied the right to stage the Games.

"When the noble qualities of the Modern Olympic Movement arose in the late nineteenth and early twentieth centuries," write the authors of *Selling the Five Rings,* an exposé of Olympic commercialism, "the founders were completely unaware of image implications, at least with regard to the consumer marketplace. Nevertheless, the images of peace, tolerance, goodwill, and noble amateur sport participation—all set in an atmosphere of high ceremony and ritual—eventually came to pay shockingly huge dividends."

The genius of classical athletics was their literal embodiment of the philosophy of the well-lived life, the pursuit of excellence, and the love of competition for its own sake. But they were practiced only by young men of aristocratic families who did not need to work for a living, which may be why Pindar and others romanticized athletes as having no "mercenary motives," only "pure love" for the training and the contest.

The genius of modern athletics is their quantum leap forward to truly international competition open to women and to every ethnic and racial group—even to physically challenged individuals, who have their own Special Olympics.

In 1996, the mayor of Thessaloniki, Konstantinos Kosmopoulos, wrote, "The Modern Olympic Games, which were first revived in Athens, symbolize the acceptance by the entire International Community of the deep-rooted values inherent in the spectacle of individual or team competition, as adapted to the needs of modern men and women . . . [They are] an expression of the desire of European politicians to base an enduring, fundamental unity on culture, and to found a permanent, rotating institution that will keep this aspiration alive."

The past hundred years have put this noble faith in the Olympics' redemptive powers to the test, as the movable feast of the modern Games has staged banquet after banquet to which the world has been invited. If we winnow the wisdom of the Olympic revival, to paraphrase historian of religion Huston Smith, there is much to be learned from each of the forty-three Summer and Winter Olympics held thus far—but not only technique and style. If we look beneath the glamour, scandals, violence, and boycotts, we can detect traces of the ancient spirit, flickers of the old fire, flares of the noble qualities that kept the ancient Games alive for twelve hundred years. But we can also discern another pattern, a kind of protean movement as the old way of playing and competing shape-shifted into one that reflects our own world.

To fully appreciate the ever-changing—yet seemingly timeless—human drama of Olympic sports in our own time, we need search for only a few *moments* from each Olympiad that personify what it means for an athlete, in Bud Greenspan's words, "to enter the arena, make the attempt, and pursue excellence." Those moments of breathtaking beauty, defiant courage, and fierce determination remind us of how the torch is passed, the fire tended, the wounded world praised. They have provided millions of people with hope and inspiration and with what sports enthusiast James Michener has called an "enlarging of the human adventure." It is to that larger adventure that we now turn.

THE GREAT SONG OF SPORTS

"What god, what hero, or what man shall we sing?" asked Pindar nearly two thousand years ago. We still wonder who is worth singing about, who we should praise, whether in song, story, or movie. This question is the long echo of our search for evidence of life's transcendent dimension and our universal celebration when we discover it.

As a young boy, I would lie awake at night clutching a transistor radio in my hand, futzing with the metal clip antenna, wiggling the earphones so I could catch the thrill of the games played by my local baseball, football, basketball, and hockey teams. On the wings of those voices from WJR in Detroit I flew, and as I heard those ball games unfold, my love for my hometown grew and my sense of identification with it intensified.

In that simple act of "rooting" for my hometown teams I was unwittingly participating in a tradition that stretches all the way back to at least ancient Olympia. Much as spectators "pulled for" athletes from their own city-states during the Olympic festival, so also peasants, city dwellers, and members of royal courts across the centuries have identified with runners, chariot racers, or ball teams and "lived or died" along with them. By rooting for my home teams I was sinking my spiritual roots, deepening my devotion to the spirit of the land I grew up on.

To this day, the gravitational force of my affection for those Detroit teams still pulls my attention to the box scores in the sports pages of the *San Francisco Chronicle*—now my local paper—and the sports pages of the *International Herald-Tribune* whenever my travels take me abroad. My heart races whenever I see the word *Detroit*, but my very soul is stirred whenever I catch a glimpse of the word *Olympics*—as if my sense of identification with one city, one state, one country widens and takes in the whole world.

My earliest memory of reading about the ancient Games goes back to a spring evening in 1967, my freshman year in high school, when I mumbled something to my parents during dinner about going out for the track team.

"Hmm," my father muttered and went on eating his Salisbury steak. "That's a good thing," he finally said. "Maybe it will give you some discipline." He arched his eyebrows and asked, "Do you know the origins of the word *athlete*?"

I rolled my eyes at my little brother, Paul, recognizing our dad's usual prelude to a lecture on the genius of the ancient Greeks. This time, though, he surprised me by asking me to follow him downstairs to the basement, where he sat me down on a chair next to the Ping-Pong table. A few minutes later he tossed a dictionary and some back issues of *National Geographic* onto the table and began to flip through them.

"Ah, I know it's in this one somewhere," he said when he found the October 1964 issue. He riffled through the pages, scoffing at the highly romanticized paintings of the ancient Games at Olympia and reminding me of the brilliant vase paintings he had pointed out at the Metropolitan Art Museum in New York a few years before. I can still recall the portrait of Phillipides, the legendary first "marathoner," who dropped dead of exhaustion when he arrived in Athens, after pronouncing his famous last statement: *Nenikikamen!* "We are victorious!" Finally, he found what he was looking for.

"Look, it's right there," he said proudly, pointing to the dictionary. "*Athlete* is from *athlos*, the ancient Greek word for 'contest.'" Then he turned to the magazine article about the then-upcoming Games in Tokyo. His voice became serious, as if he was about to get down and dirty in a big football game. "Here, this is what you are getting yourself into, Son, a dog-eat-dog world where everything is a contest. But if you learn how to compete, you'll do well for yourself. That's why sports are important: they teach you how to deal with adversity, how to rise above yourself, how to believe in yourself."

That moment glows in my memory. I remember the longing in my father's voice for me to understand that there is a great and noble history behind virtually everything that we do. That's why we read the classics together as a family and why he often spent his winter evenings in the basement creating scrapbooks for his family, filling them with clippings from travel articles and art magazines, along with photographs of trains, planes, and ships, movie stars, inventors, and sports heroes.

Looking back, I'm convinced my father was trying, in his own way, to pass the torch of inspiration to me. I thought of his effort recently when reading about Sydney Mills, a poor Oglala Sioux man on the Pine Ridge Reservation, South Dakota, who was determined that his son find and follow his dream to a better life than his own. To do this, Mills assembled a scrapbook for his boy, filled with paintings and stories of the great warrior Crazy Horse and newspaper clippings about Olympic champions.

"Olympians are chosen by the gods," Sydney told his son, Billy, and those words burned in the boy for the rest of his life as he fought hard to overcome racial prejudice, poverty, obscurity, and the death of both his parents.

At Mill's induction into the World Sports Humanitarian Hall of Fame, author Nicholas Sparks said, "He took up running to escape the pain and emptiness he felt inside. As he once put it, 'I was a mixed blood and an orphan. You couldn't get much lonelier that that.'"

When Billy Mills discovered running, he discovered his dream. After setting several long-distance records at the University of Kansas, he joined the Marines and began training for the 15,000-meter race at the 1964 Tokyo Games. He captured the spirit of the Olympic ideal in his training notebook when he wrote, "Believe! Believe! Believe!" He then fulfilled his Olympic dream when he ran (in borrowed shoes) as a virtual unknown in one of the most illustrious races in the Games' history.

His story is the stuff of modern myth: the passing of the torch of inspiration from generation to generation, the ferocious fire that burns in the heart to prove ourselves to an indifferent world, and then the desire to pass the torch on.

LET THE GAMES RESUME

After the surprising success of the 1896 Athens Games, the Olympic movement meandered its way into the twentieth century. The ideals of fair play and democratization of the playing field were eventually embraced, as reflected in the rich variety of Olympic athletes' professions. Olympic scholar David Wallechinsky lists an extraordinary range of jobs: sign painter, dentist, bricklayer, butcher's apprentice, student teacher, artillery officer, carpenter, plumber, mechanic, death-marcher, rancher, nurse, clerk, spinning-mill worker, aviation engineer, deep-sea diver, policeman, bus driver, and—my personal favorites—a typewriter mechanic and a chicken sexer.

However, the ancient dream of international brotherhood accomplished through athletic competition, and the belief in the Games as a force for peace, were challenged by the belligerent realities of political and commercial exploitation. It was in part to counteract these frenzied forces of nationalism that Coubertin had sought to restore the ancient Greek athletic program and revive the natural sense of pride in one's own nation. His vision paralleled that of Greece's ancient rulers. He dreamed of encouraging identification with one's homeland—but not at the expense of another's—and illustrating again and again (every four years) that human beings can be peacefully competitive. His insistence on worldwide sites was meant to foster a sense of equality among nations, as well as to stimulate curiosity about each people. But his vision was as deep as it was wide, as spiritual and artistic as it was practical and political.

As Susan Wels writes in *The Olympic Spirit*, "He also sought to rekindle the Greek spiritual connection between art and sport. The universal messages of the Games, Coubertin saw, needed to be communicated through artistic symbols and ceremony, such as the dramatic flight of doves that opened the very first modern Games in Athens in 1896. In that spirit, other icons and rituals followed."

To accomplish this dream, Coubertin included a clause in the Olympic charter suggesting that cultural events "of an equal standard" be offered along with the athletic events. He also organized a conference in Paris in 1906 to implement the encyclopedic approach of the ancient Greeks. "The conference," writes Dil, "recommended that . . . the Olympics should include official competitions in five aesthetic areas: architecture, sculpture, painting, music, and literature. Quadrennial prizes would be awarded for the best new works that found their inspiration in sport."

Coubertin's panoramic vision was put into play at the 1912 Games in Stockholm and continued until the 1948 London Games, when official competitions in artistic fields were suspended. However, they have continued unofficially in the form of art exhibitions, music compositions, ceremonial openings and closings, and architectural works that have complemented many modern Olympic festivals.

As Huston Smith told me in a recent interview, "When ceremonies really work they do more than celebrate, they *discover* and *achieve*. What they discover is the sacred dimension that is often hidden; what they achieve is a moment of transcendence. That is to say, the ceremony points to what is divine in the world." It is in this ceremonial spirit of celebration and transcendence of the political tensions that had plagued nineteenth-century Europe that the Games were revived; but keeping them above and beyond the reach of politics would prove an ordeal, an endurance test, and an ethics exam for every host city for the next hundred years. Nevertheless, Coubertin's essential dream of an "athletic renaissance" can now be regarded as what he boldly predicted it would be: one of the milestones of the nineteenth century.

Despite a concerted effort by the Greeks to establish a "stable and permanent" home for the modern Olympics in their native land, Coubertin persuaded the nascent International Olympic Committee to stage the second Olympiad in his own hometown. They were held in 1900, but only half-heartedly, as a kind of sideshow to the Paris World's Fair. Several new events were added, including boxing, polo, archery, and soccer, but these were overshadowed by the peculiar addition of more than twenty shooting contests—including one involving live pigeons—a tug-of-war competition, and an all-around dumb-bell contest. The one and only croquet competition in Olympic history was also staged, witnessed by exactly *one* fan, an Englishman, who saw the French sweep the medals.

On the up side, the Olympic ideal now included women for the first time. Charlotte Cooper from Great Britain holds the distinction of being crowned the first woman Olympic champion. On July 11, 1900, she defeated Helene Prevost of France to win the tennis competition. But because the Games were drawn out for five months and were so badly organized, some athletes did not even realize they were participating in Olympic competition. The winner of the women's golf competition, American Margaret Abbott, believed until her death in 1955 that she had simply competed in a local tournament.

If there had been an Olympic spirit award that year, it would have gone to an American standing jumper who had spent his childhood in a wheelchair, partially paralyzed by polio. Fortunately, the boy, Ray Ewry, was cared for by a doctor who had recommended agonizing but effective jumping exercises to make his legs stronger, and he had unfailingly performed them. Nicknamed "Deac" because he was studying to become a deacon, "the Rubber Man" because of his suppleness, and "the Human Frog" for his uncanny ability to spring from a crouching position, Ewry won three events—the standing high jump, standing broad jump, and standing triple jump—in Paris. Over the span of three Olympiads—in 1900, 1904, and 1908—Ewry won eight gold medals in standing jump events. Ewry took home more golds from the Intercalary Athenian Olympic Games in

1906. No one has ever won more, so Ewry's record still stands, so to speak. His specialty events were discontinued after the Stockholm Games of 1912. The photographs of his astonishing standing leaps reveal him as a coiled spring in gym shorts. They are portraits of courage and determination—and the irrepressible human desire to *jump*.

The deeply moving images of Ewry bring to mind the marvelous collection of *Jump!* photographs of illustrious actors, diplomats, and comedians by famed portraitist Philippe Halsman.

Ray Ewry showing his famous springing, scissors-style high-jump. London, 1908.

He writes in the accompanying essay, "In a jump, the subject, in a sudden burst of energy, overcomes gravity. He cannot simultaneously control his expressions, his facial and limb muscles. The mask falls. The real self becomes visible." Much as myth involves the masking and unmasking of gods, Olympic sport involves the masking of superb athletes through intense media coverage, and, occasionally, the unmasking of them during the white heat of performance or under the klieg light of the postcompetition interview, when the "real self" emerges and captures the hearts of people around the world. In that spirit, when basketball star Julius Irving was asked the secret of his gravity defeating jumps, he said he was "leaping for God."

The St. Louis World's Fair of 1904 is famous for introducing the hot dog, the ice cream cone, and the song later memorialized by Judy Garland, "Meet Me in St. Louis." It was described as "a fair where there are also sports," a cavalier reference to the Olympic Games that helps explain the hapless planning and the poor attendance by athletes. Only thirteen countries sent teams. The others decided not to risk sending their athletes on the long ocean cruise followed by a thousand-mile train ride through countryside many feared was still riddled with dangerous Indians.

Once the Games got under way, the American athletes fared well. They were led again by Ray Ewry; Archie Hahn, "the Milwaukee Meteor," who won the 60-meter, 100-meter, and 200-meter sprints; the delightfully named James Lightbody, who broke the world records in the 800-meter and 1,500-meter races; and a sixty-eight-year-old Civil War veteran, Samuel Duvall, who won a bronze medal as a member of the American archery team.

However, the reputation of the 1904 Games will be forever marred by the so-called Anthropological Games. Under the pretense of science, "exotic ethnic groups" or so-called primitive peoples, such as Pygmies, Patagonians, Filipinos, Moros, Oglala

Sioux, Cocopans, and Ainus, were studied. The conceit was concern about whether "savages" could compete with Europeans and Americans in sprints and hurdling, or in the shot put, as an African Pygmy was compelled to do. Native sports that were staged included mud fighting, dart throwing, a greased-pole climb, and a bow-and-arrow shooting contest.

A tug-of-war between the Oglala Sioux and Arapahoe tribes, as part of the infamous "Anthropology Days" competition during the 1904 Olympics.

Coubertin, who did not attend, commented that such a spectacle could only have happened in America. "Such an event, so contrary to the Olympic ideal, could hardly have been held anywhere else in the world other than on this frontier of the southern states ... As for that outrageous charade, it will, of course, lose its appeal when black men, red men, and yellow men learn to run, jump, and throw and leave the white men behind them."

Nevertheless, if the chronicles of the 1904 Games are read closely, it is still possible to discover displays of Olympic spirit during the five months of competition in St. Louis. According to Olympic historian Tom Ecker, a Cuban mail carrier and marathon runner named Felix Carvajal raised the money to travel to Missouri "with a daily routine of running laps around the town-square in Havana ... and asking for contributions to send him to the Olympics." When he reached New Orleans he lost all his travel money and athletic gear in a dice game, so he hitchhiked and ran all the way to St. Louis. He still managed to compete, running in cutoff trousers and street shoes, stopping "to chat with spectators and practice his English." Unwisely, he picked some green apples from an orchard and after eating them was hit by a terrible case of cramps—but with admirable perseverance he kept going and managed a fourth place finish.

Already in the first few Olympiads a remarkable "pattern of meaning" was being established. It was the modern parallel to the ancient pursuit of excellence—what Olympic swimmer John Naber would later call the fans' affection for "stories of determination." Or as Vince Lombardi was fond of reminding his players, "The real glory is being knocked to your knees and then coming back. That's real glory. That's the essence of it."

RESTORING THE RITUALS

The International Olympic Committee (IOC) agreed to Coubertin's plan to reinforce the mythic atmosphere surrounding the Games by staging them in Rome in 1908, "as an international homage to Roman antiquity." After the recent debacle, Coubertin said, "I desired Rome only because I wanted Olympism, after its return from utilitarian America, to don once again the sumptuous toga, woven of art and philosophy, in which I had always wanted to clothe her." His grand plans to resuscitate the flagging fortunes of the Games included erecting athlete statues all over the city; staging car races in Milan, wrestling in the Colosseum, and nautical battles in the Bay of Naples; and reviving competitions in art and drama. Inauspiciously, the eruption of Mount Vesuvius in 1906 plunged Italy into economic chaos, and the IOC was forced to change the Games' venue.

Remarkably, London agreed to a swift transfer of the Games. They were held in Shepherd's Bush Stadium, and despite the presence of another World's Fair unfolding around them and a plethora of protests about the quality of the judging, the Olympics staged by the British were impressive.

In contrast to the ancient Games, which rarely accommodated innovations, Coubertin encouraged modernizing of the revived Games. But the changes he proposed grew out of a deeply felt belief that ritual and ceremony were indispensable, if the Games were to stand out from ordinary athletic competition and eventually be regarded with as much reverence and respect as the festival at Olympia.

At London, gold medals were handed out for the first time—far more ceremonial than the umbrellas, books, and porcelain cups given to victors at the Paris Games. The London Games also featured the publishing of the Olympic Creed, plus a change in the opening ceremony that marked a significant break with the past. During the procession of athletes past King Edward VII, the flag bearers from each nation were expected to dip their flags, as an act of ritual respect. However, one lone athlete refused to do so. An American shot-put champion, Ralph Rose, winner of three gold medals, two silvers, and one bronze over the course of his stellar Olympic career, did not lower the Stars and Stripes. His refusal was not an act of *disrespect* to the king but was out of respect for the democratic and Olympic ideals that all are equal in the eyes of God. His teammate and fellow shot-putter Martin Sheridan, gold medal winner in the 1906 Athens Games, later uttered the now-legendary words: "The flag dips for no earthly king."

Since then, none have.

The London Games also marked the establishment of an official distance for the marathon, one of the most glamorous and popular modern events. The story goes that the IOC declared an even twenty-six miles as the distance, in honor of Phillipides' triumphant run along the Marathon road to Athens. But King Edward requested that the marathon begin on the road that passed by the nursery at Windsor Castle, so his grandchildren could see the start of the race, and end in front of the royal box at the Olympic Stadium in London, so Queen Alexandra might view the finish. The royal request is the reason why 385 yards were tacked onto the twenty six miles. The IOC conceded.

Official records list American Johnny Hayes as the first victor at this now universal distance. But it was Dorando Pietri, a young candy maker from Capri, Italy, who captured the world's imagination. The dramatic photographs and scratchy film footage of the dreadfully exhausted Pietri entering the stadium first—then turning in the wrong direction—seemed to confirm the public's preconception of valiant effort being at the heart of Olympic competition.

Described by a British journalist as "dizzy with excitement, devastated by the utmost atrocities of fatigue, but indomitable, still . . . the wretched man fell down, incapable of going on for the two hundred yards that alone separated him from the winning post in front of the royal box. He was lifted up, and fell again. He struggled pitifully along to within fifty yards of the finish and collapsed."

At that point Pietri was grabbed and pointed in the right direction, then actually dragged across the finish line by a brace of well-meaning men, including the Clerk of the Course and Sir Arthur Conan Doyle, of Sherlock Holmes fame. One official explained their interference by saying, "It was impossible to leave him there, for it looked as if he might die in the very presence of the Queen."

Their spontaneous gesture may have saved the life of Pietri, who was later described as being at death's door with his heart half an inch out of place. But the compassion for his condition did not extend to stretching the rules. He was disqualified for being helped across the finish line; however, the queen awarded him a special gold cup for his spirit and courage the following day. The combination of royal recognition and public fascination with acts of indomitable will power made Pietri an overnight sensation and set off a worldwide fad for running marathons.

However, things aren't always as they seem. Olympic filmmaker Bud Greenspan adds an odd footnote to Dorando's story. A member of a gold-medal-winning relay team at the London Games, Joe Deakin, came forward at the age of ninety-one to say that he had seen the race's controversial finish. "The problem was," said Deakin, "that people along the way were giving him glasses of Chantilly instead of water. Pietri wasn't exhausted. He was drunk."

For many, the 1912 Stockholm Games were the saving grace of the Olympic movement, so much so that Coubertin declared them an "enchantment." They also featured technological innovations, such as worldwide press coverage, a public address system, and electronic timing. Three of the most popular athletes were Native Americans. The legendary Hawaiian swimmer Duke Kahanamoku brought along his Hawaiian crawl and flutter kick and won the 100-meter freestyle. The pride of the Hopis, Lewis Tewanima, won a bronze medal in the 10,000-meter footrace. But it was Jim Thorpe, the All-American football player and track star, part Sac and part Fox Indian, part Irish and part French, who startled the sporting world. First, Thorpe, who was called Wa-Tho-Huck, or Bright Path, by his own tribe, won the demanding pentathlon; the next day he placed fourth in the high jump and seventh in the long jump; and the following day he won the decathlon—an unprecedented feat.

© IOC/Olympic Museum Collections

*The immortal Jim Thorpe, voted the Greatest Male
Athlete of the first half of the 20th century.*

When King Gustav V of Sweden handed Thorpe his medals,
he remarked, "Sir, you are the greatest athlete in the world."

Thorpe replied simply and humbly, "Thanks, King."

Returning home from his terrific triumph, he was treated
like a national hero, honored with a ticker tape parade in New
York City. Shortly afterward, an IOC committee was formed to
deal with violations of the arbitrarily enforced amateur laws.
When it was discovered that Thorpe had played semiprofession-
al baseball for a summer, this was considered a violation of his

amateur status. That status was promptly stripped from him; his medals and prizes were seized and his records stricken.

Thorpe's self-defense survives in his appeal letter to the international officials: "I will be partly excused by the fact that I was simply an Indian schoolboy and did not know all about such things. I did not play for the money. I played because I liked baseball."

Four decades later, in 1950, Thorpe was named the greatest athlete of the half century because of his stunning performances in the Olympics and his heroics in professional football and baseball, but also because of his well-known self-defense, which underscored the purity of his motives. In the 1941 film *The Jim Thorpe Story*, he was portrayed by the brooding young actor Burt Lancaster.

The great baseball player Ed Roush related an exchange he once had with Thorpe: "'Jim, anybody in those Olympic games ever make you really run your best?' 'I never yet saw the man I couldn't look back at,' he says to me. I believed him."

The subtle strength of those words goes to the heart of the Jim Thorpe myth. His story reveals our ambivalence towards raw, pure talent, the fire in the belly that stokes great athletes. And most poignantly, it shows the damage that can be wrought by misplaced mythological thinking—like the forced ideal of amateurism as a standard for participation in the Olympics, although it never existed in the ancient Games. Thorpe's medals, plus a bust of King Gustav and a silver chalice shaped like a Viking ship, that had been taken from him were sent to Lausanne, Switzerland, where they sat on the shelves of the IOC headquarters. They became, in the words of Olympic historian William Oscar Johnson, "a symbol of what happened to a naïve young Native American caught in the clutches of the self-righteous puritans who ran 'amateur' athletics in those days."

One of the most unwavering advocates of amateurism was Avery Brundage, president of the IOC from 1936 to 1972, who refused repeated efforts to reinstate Thorpe's records. His critics claim a serious conflict of interest, since Brundage had competed against and lost to Thorpe in the decathlon and pentathlon at Stockholm.

Finally, in 1982, the International Olympic Committee reinstated Thorpe's records, though they declared him only "co-winner" of the decathlon and pentathlon. His medals were returned to his children; he had died years before, in 1953, alone and embittered, in a trailer park in Lomita, California.

THE REENCHANTMENT OF THE GAMES

Due to the outbreak of World War I, the Sixth Olympiad, planned for Berlin, was canceled. Wallechinsky notes the tragic irony: "In ancient times, all wars were suspended during the period of the Olympics. In modern times, the reverse has been true."

In recognition of the sacrifices that the Belgians had made during World War I, the 1920 Games were awarded to Antwerp. The resumption of the Games was a grim reminder of the Olympic movement's failure as an arbiter in the issue of war and peace. The Axis powers—Germany, Austria, Bulgaria, Hungary, and Turkey—were disinvited and not allowed to participate, but twenty-nine other nations took part in the hope of rallying the spirits of their citizenry.

In accord with the Olympic movement's irrepressible idealism, Coubertin added several ceremonial innovations at the Antwerp Games. The first was the Olympic flag with its five interlocked rings, which the baron claimed was based upon an inscription he discovered on a stone block among the ruins of ancient Delphi. The five circles, he announced, represented the linking together of the ancient and modern Olympics through the linking in brotherhood of all nations on the five continents. This was meant to be underscored by the rings' colors—red, blue, yellow, green, and black—at least one of which is found on the flag of every nation around the world. The baron further instructed that the mayor of the Olympic host city should personally hand over the flag to the mayor of the next host city during the festival's closing ceremonies.

However, Young believes this was nothing more than "an especially beguiling myth" perpetrated by Coubertin. In an essay for *Archaeology* magazine in 1996, he states that Coubertin had origin-ally intended each ring to represent one of the first five Olympiads—those that had preceded the Antwerp Games—with another ring to be added with each new Olympiad. When the First World War led to cancellation of the 1916 Games, Young writes, "Coubertin gave the symbol a different official meaning."

Another of Coubertin's 1920 innovations that has lasted to this day is the Olympic oath, which an athlete from the host country recites, while clutching a corner of the Olympic flag, during the opening ceremony. The first athlete to be so honored was Belgian fencer Victor Boin. The original oath read:

> In the name of all competitors I promise that we shall take part in the Olympic Games, respecting and abiding by the rules which govern them, in the true spirit of sportsmanship, for the glory of sport and the honor of our countries.

Chastened by two world wars and the ongoing Cold War, however, in the 1950s the IOC eliminated the reference to "our countries" out of concern that it would encourage nationalism at the Games.

Coubertin's third innovation at the Antwerp Games was the Olympic motto: *Citius, altius, fortius,* meaning "Swifter, higher, stronger." He later credited the motto to Father Henri

Martin Didon, a French Dominican friar. He had heard Didon use the Latin phrase with his students at Arcueil College in hopes that it would build "the sporting spirit of his pupils."

Beyond its pageantry, the 1920 Games boasted a colorful cast of characters, including American sprinter Charley Paddock, famed for his flamboyant, lunging finishes, the first runner to be called "the world's fastest human." Italian champion marathoner Valerio Arri was so exultant about coming in third place, just behind the "Flying Finn," Hannes Kolehmainen, in first place and Juri Lossmann of Estonia in second, that he turned three cartwheels as soon as he crossed the finish line. Great Britain's Albert Hill, a veteran of the First World War, took the gold in the 800-meter and 1,500-meter races, while the silver in the 1,500 was won by his fellow countryman Philip Noel-Baker, who later served in Parliament for over three decades. Baker was awarded the Nobel Peace Prize in 1959 for his passionate dedication to the cause of nuclear disarmament.

These Games also featured the grimly determined Finn Paavo Nurmi, winner of the 10,000-meter and cross-country races. In the absence of any solid information about him rumors abounded, including the marvelous story that he had learned how to run by racing the local mail train, and talk that he subsisted on a diet of only oatmeal, black bread, and fish. His own innovation—the tactic of pacing himself with a stopwatch—both inspired and troubled people in an era when the robot was becoming symbolic of the modern soulless human being. One contemporary newspaperman wrote, "He's a mechanical Frankenstein created to annihilate time."

As floating filaments of metal are attracted to a magnet, so too are drifting shreds of truth absorbed into sports legends. The times needed a myth to express the tension accompanying the lower classes' often humiliating and gradual inclusion into upper-class competitions such as the Olympics. The story of

Jack B. Kelly afforded just that. It described Kelly as an unheralded, poor, but scrupulously hardworking man from Philadelphia who was snubbed by the Henley Royal Regatta in his attempt to enter a single sculls race. In reality, Kelly was the owner of a brick company and the premier oarsman of his time, though he was indeed rejected by the Henley club. Despite the rejection, Kelly went on to win 126 straight races, including an Olympic race in the single sculls—over Jack Beresford, the Henley champion. Later in life, Kelly raised a family that included the future Princess of Monaco, Grace Kelly, and a son, Jack Jr., who brandished a bronze medal after the 1956 Melbourne Games.

Legend has it that after his victory in Antwerp, he sent his kelly green racing cap to King George V, along with a letter that said only "Greetings from a bricklayer."

As the newspaperman says at the shadowy end of *Who Shot Liberty Valance?* "When in doubt, print the legend."

Much to the delight of Baron de Coubertin and his fellow countrymen who had been supporting the Olympic movement, the Games returned to Paris in 1924. The mid-twenties were *les annees folles,* "the crazy years" of Paris, the middle of the jazz age, and the world seemed ready to celebrate a truly international sports festival. A record forty-four nations attended, but the competitions were plagued by numerous complaints from visitors about the provincialism of local fans—a distant echo of ancient Greek class-consciousness. Despite their own boorish booing of other national anthems, French spectators severely caned an American art student for his "rooting," a demonstrative, noisy behavior that they found uncivilized.

As any photographic compilation of Olympic history will reveal, the star of the Paris Games was the young swimming phenom Johnny Weismuller. As an immigrant from Romania, he had been forced to learn how to protect himself in the fierce world of New York street gangs. According to *Tarzan's Son*, Johnny Weissmuller Jr.'s autobiography, Weissmuller Sr. trained himself to be tough through sports. "My father was once quoted as saying, 'Before swimming, there was nothing . . . only surviving.'"

At the Paris Games, the future Tarzan of the movies swam his way to three gold victories, including the 100-meter freestyle, where he outsprinted his arch rival, the "invincible" Duke Kahanamoku; the 400-meter freestyle, where he shattered the world record by 40 seconds; and the 4 x 200 freestyle relay as a member of the winning team. He also won a bronze as part of the American water polo team. Eventually, Weissmuller would hold sixty-seven different world records; but he remained unruffled by the fame and glamour that came with such accomplishments. "Even as a kid I never tensed up," Weissmuller said. "Not even the Olympics fazed me."

Two other 1924 Olympians were later mythologized for their performances in Paris: the raffish Englishman Harold Abrahams and the affable American champion Jackson Scholz. The two sprinters finished first and second, respectively, in the 100-meter dash and, along with 400-meter champion Eric Liddell, were glorified in the movie *Chariots of Fire*. The movie's title is lifted from William Blake's mystical poem:

> Bring me my bow of burning gold!
> Bring me my arrows of delight!
> Bring me my spear! O cloud, unfold!
> Bring me my chariots of fire!

Despite the festive air, the numerous world records, and the rousing public reception, there were a few melodramatic cat-calls from the press in both Europe and the United States, declaring the 1924 Games a sham and blatantly nationalistic. Nevertheless, Coubertin retired the following year in a buoyant mood. He blithely expressed confidence about the future of the Games. "My work is done," he said. "The world institution that we have built up is ready to face any eventualities."

In 1928, the very first Winter Olympics were staged, in Chamonix, France, under the name "International Winter Sports Week." The Games featured competitions in ice hockey, figure skating, speed skating, ski jumping, and cross-country skiing. One athlete soared above all: the diminutive Norwegian, fifteen-year-old Sonja Henie, whose balletlike program of leaps and spins and daring short-skirt costumes not only led to the first of her three gold medals in figure skating but revolutionized the sport. Henie turned professional after the 1936 Berlin Games and became popular in ice shows and movies, making her, according to Greenspan, "the most commercially successful Olympic champion in history." But as is often the case with Olympic champions, Henie's real legacy is subtler. Her gift to skating was the utter joy she displayed on the ice, her proud display of erotic beauty, and her feminine strength, which inspired millions of young women to lace up skates and follow in her gliding footsteps.

Six months later, the Ninth Olympiad was held in Amsterdam. Several more rituals and ceremonies were added to deepen the emphasis on the true spirit of the Games and strengthen the sense of international brotherhood through fair play and competition.

The first Olympic flame was lit, to burn for the duration of the festival; and despite Coubertin's and Pope Pius XI's objections, female athletes appeared for the first time in track and field events. Women had previously competed in tennis, golf, archery, figure skating, yachting, swimming, and fencing, but it was feared they could not withstand the rigors of racing. When several women collapsed from exhaustion at the end of the

800-meter race, the IOC, in a case of mean-spirited interpretation, banned women from racing at that distance. The event wasn't reinstated until thirty-two years later.

In *The Olympics,* Allen Guttman explains the peculiar projection of weakness onto women and the long bias against them: "Hysterical fears of 'Amazons' with 'masculine development' was one bugaboo that haunted the nineteenth and early twentieth century. A related fear was that strenuous sports competition was certain to destroy a girl's health and make her forever unfit to become a mother. In short, the criteria for middle-class women's physical activity were hygenic and aesthetic rather than athletic."

Despite the dark shadows cast upon the women's competition, one young woman shone brightly. The Riverdale, Illinois, high school track coach had recruited Betty Robinson for the school's team when he watched her running to catch up with a train he was riding on. "He suggested that I should develop my talent. Till then I didn't even know there were women's races." Sixteen-year-old Robinson beat Canadian Fanny Rosenfeld in the 100-meters—making her the official first female gold-medal winner in track—and then a silver medal in the 800-meters, and later another gold in the 4 x 100 relay.

Not only did Robinson defy the patronizing pundits of sports, three years later she defied death itself. In 1931, she was nearly killed in a plane crash. For seven weeks she lay unconscious, having suffered a concussion, severe lacerations, and a broken leg. It took her two years to be able to walk again. Yet she became one of destiny's darlings by returning to training with tenacity and eventually competing again. In the 1936 Games she won another gold medal, as part of the American 4 x 100-meter relay team.

Another female athlete who stole the hearts of the spectators at the Amsterdam Games was "the Saskatoon Lily," eighteen-year-old Ethel Catherwood, a Canadian high jumper who won the gold medal with a leap of 5 feet, 2½ inches. Her combination of exceptional talent and dazzling good looks was an echo of the ancient Greek ideal, as memorialized in the Olympic victor statue that bears the inscription: "Where beauty and strength unite." In the modern world that combination is also irresistible to the marketing mavens of Hollywood, who immediately came knocking on Catherwood's door. She refused their offers, saying, "I'd rather gulp poison than try my hand at motion pictures." Her triumphant return to Saskatoon was as heroic as that of any athlete from ancient times, triggering the greatest party in the city since the end of the First World War.

The men's competitions in Amsterdam were again dominated by the indefatigable Paavo Nurmi and the man who claimed he never lost a swimming race, "not even at the YMCA"—Johnny Weissmuller. Nurmi was victorious in the 10,000 meters and achieved second-place finishes in the 5,000 meters and the 3,000-meter steeplechase. Weismuller streaked to a new Olympic record in the 100-meter crawl and won again in the 200-meter relay. Together, they seemed to represent the two sides of ancient drama, the Dionysian and the Apollonian—Nurmi as the god of agonizing death and triumphant rebirth, and Weismuller swimming with apparent godlike effortlessness and radiating a kind of luminous confidence.

Watching Johnny Weismuller in vintage Olympics film footage reminds me of poet Robert Francis's wonderful lines in "Swimmer": "Observe how he negotiates his way / With trust and the least violence, making / The stranger friend, the enemy ally." Together, athlete and poet evoke the Olympic spirit of sublimating the violent streak in human nature through a peaceful harnessing of the body's energy in harmony with nature's rhythms, and reveal the still point within movement.

The Depression of 1929 took a rapacious toll both economically and spiritually on the entire world, and the need for diversion and inspiration grew proportionately. In Hollywood, escapist and class-struggle movies became popular, while attention to sports stars reached a new level of intensity and expectation. The lines between popular entertainment, show business, and sports began to blur. By the early 1930s, the combination of economic woes and drumbeats of war triggered demands that the next Olympiad, in 1932, be cancelled. It was the old tug-of-war between "realists," who viewed the Olympics as trivial and a dissipation of national energies, and "idealists," who saw the Games as a life-affirming ritual, a source of optimism and possible peacemaking.

The Los Angeles Olympic Committee was not to be denied.

"The spirit and tenacity of William May Garland and his fellow Los Angeles organizers," writes Tom Ecker, "and the support of the world's Olympic committees prevailed. Los Angeles was able to stage the first of the expensive, highly-organized spectacles that have since typified the Olympics." The economic pressures of the Depression, now in full swing, meant that far fewer athletes were able to travel and compete. But far more watched than ever before, partly because the Games were held in the appropriately named Coliseum, which held over 100,000 spectators.

The 1932 Los Angeles Games became known as the "Hollywood Games," with as many movie stars, like Clark Gable and Jean Harlow, in the stands as there were Olympic legends like Jim Thorpe and Duke Kahanamoku, which lent the Olympics a new cachet. "It was like a fantasyland," sighed Evelyne Hall, a hurdler from Chicago. "Nobody thought about their problems."

The caliber of competition was excellent, highlighted by Babe Didrikson's spectacular performance and the emergence of another future Tarzan in the swimming events, Buster Crabbe, who took the 400-meter crown in record time. The great Italian cyclist Attilio Pavesi earned two gold medals, emboldened by a hearty lunch of pasta, pastry, and sandwiches tucked inside his racing uniform. However, an especially spirited competition in the discus, led by John Anderson's throw of 162 feet, 4 inches, left a deeper impression than America's sweep of medals.

Since the Games were being held during Prohibition, no alcohol was permitted in the Olympic Village. The French team nevertheless lobbied for an exception, arguing that wine was vital to their athletes' diet. Their discus thrower, Jules Noel, took advantage of the special permission and was seen repeatedly "swigging champagne with his compatriots" in the locker room. Under the mythic influence of Dionysus, the god of the vine, Noel paid enough attention to hurl an apparently medal-winning throw on his fourth attempt—but the officials weren't paying the same quality of attention. They were distracted by the pole vault competition and missed the throw. The Frenchman was allowed an extra throw but was unable to match his previous one and finished fourth, behind the sober Americans.

The Los Angeles organizers' persistence was vindicated by their staging the first profitable Olympic festival. Yet the 1932 Games were also aesthetically satisfying enough to inspire legendary sportswriter Grantland Rice to call them the "greatest sporting pageant in world history."

TESTING THE OLYMPIC SPIRIT

"In Germany," writes biographer Milly Mogulof, "the Olympic spirit was sorely tested." Adolf Hitler at first resisted even staging the 1936 Berlin Games, remarking that the Olympic vision was nothing more than "an invention of Jews and

Freemasons." But he relented—and then attempted to use the Games as "a virtual festival of propaganda" for his theories of Aryan supremacy. The disturbing reports of Nazi persecution of Jews ignited impassioned calls for a boycott, on grounds that staging the Games in a country with such policies would have meant "offending the true spirit of the Games," as one American judge wrote. Furthermore, as David B. Kanin comments, the boycott movement disdained the Nazi official stance that "chivalry, sportsmanship, and fair play [are] the vices of the weak rather than the virtues of the strong and which [rejected] Christianity for paganism and [repudiated] the principle of equality upon which both political and sport are based, for the dogma of the superiority of the Aryans to all people."

However, German officials persuaded IOC president Avery Brundage to allow the Games to go forward, on the premise that Jewish athletes would be allowed to participate. "I don't think we have any business to meddle in this question," Brundage said, rationalizing his decision to go forward. "We are a sports group, organized and pledged to promote clean competition and sportsmanship. When we let politics, racial questions, religious or social disputes creep into our actions, we're in for trouble."

With the ill-fated Hindenberg flying overhead and over a hundred thousand spectators singing "Deutchland über alles," the Games began in haunting fashion. The one truly stunning innovation was the unveiling of the Olympic torch relay—the inspiration of Carl Diem, organizer of the Games, who was seeking to "glamorize them with an ancient aura." The torch had been constructed by the Krupp firm, then lit in the Temple of Hera in Olympia, then carried by three thousand different runners before arriving at the Berlin Stadium. It was carried up the steep steps to a massive cauldron, where it burned for the remainder of the festival.

As moving a spectacle as it was, the real fire of the Games proved to be in the hearts and souls of the athletes who competed in the spirit of the ancients, believing that the Olympics might momentarily transcend the follies of politics. This hope and determination were personified in Jesse Owens. Although personally torn by the specter of Berlin, which he called "a godless city," and hurt when Nazis called him one of America's "black auxiliaries," Owens was determined to compete.

"The purpose of the Olympics, anyway," he wrote later, "was to do your best. As I'd learned from [coach] Charles Riley, the only victory that counts is the one over yourself."

Also caught in the vise of international politics was Jewish fencer Helene Meyer, gold-medal winner at the 1928 Amsterdam Games. Described by Milly Mogulof as a blonde beauty seen as the embodiment of German womanhood, she was so beloved that millions of porcelain statues of her were bought for display in homes across Germany. After her bronze-medal performance at the Los Angeles Games, she was driven by a ferocious desire to win back the title of greatest fencer in the world and was lured back home by the Nazis as their "token Jewish athlete." Yet Meyer's return performance became a sordid tale. "She yearned for her rebirth as an authentic German and a fencer par excellence," writes Mogulof, but neither happened. Meyer lost her final match to finish in second place, behind another Jewess, Ilona Elek, from Hungary. She never recovered from what she viewed as a defeat. She lived the rest of her life in exile in California, a symbol of the ambivalent forces that drive an athlete's soul to be reborn through sport alone.

One of the most luminous lessons of sportsmanship in Olympic history was captured by Leni Riefenstahl in the pole vault competition sequence of her now-legendary film on the Berlin Games, *Olympia*. The brilliant black-and-white footage shows a series of pole vaulters flinging through the fading late afternoon light like flip cards being rapidly thumbed. One by one they are eliminated as darkness slowly cloaks the stadium, until only three sinuously strong vaulters are left. Under the eerie illumination of a handful of floodlights, one American, Earle Meadows, and two good friends from Japan, Shuhei Nishida and Sueo Oe, carry on valiantly as they soar higher and higher into the blue-black sky. Finally, the bar is placed at 14 feet, 3¼ inches. Meadows sails over it on his second attempt, but neither Nishida and Oe can match him in their three attempts each. In the spirit of good sportsmanship, they race over to shake his hand.

Unfazed, smiling, and proud, they continued to jump for the silver and bronze medal until the officials suspended the competition on account of darkness and the late hour. For reasons still unknown, the next day Nishida was awarded the silver (his second) and Oe the bronze, which is what they wore on the victory stand.

When they arrived home in Japan, however, they decided they were not happy with the officials' arbitrary decision. They commissioned a jeweler to cut the two medals lengthwise, rearrange the pieces, then solder them back together so each of them owned a medal that was half silver and half bronze. The medals have taken on a life of their own; they are housed now at the National Stadium in Tokyo under the name "Medals of Eternal Friendship."

As the sign in Einstein's office said, "Not everything that can be counted counts, and not everything that counts can be counted." What counted to Nishida and Oe was shared glory and long friendship; what didn't count was allowing chance to determine their fame and fortune.

After a twelve-year suspension of the Games due to the horrors that ravaged the Continent during World War II, the Olympics were staged once again in "the austerity Games," in

London in 1948. The war's aggressors, Germany and Japan, were not invited, and the Olympic arts competitions were staged for the final time. A superb athlete who has come to personify the spirit of those Games is Francina "Fanny" Blankers-Koen, "the Flying House-wife" from Holland. Although she had competed in the Berlin Games as an eighteen-year-old high jumper, her career was nearly snuffed out by the long hiatus. In the meantime she had married her coach and borne two children. When the "austerity Games" in London approached, she was thirty years of age and the world-record holder in all her events. But rather than being lauded for talent and determination by her fellow Dutch, she was ridiculed for evading her responsibilities as a mother. Yet her own mind was clear, and her heart was fired with determination to do well; she defied convention and competed in London. With her father willingly taking care of the children—and promising to dance around the kitchen table if she triumphed—Blankers-Koen dashed her way to victory in her first two events, the 100-meter and the 80-meter hurdles.

But the competition was taking its toll. Moments before the semifinal heat of the 200 meters, she told her husband she was ready to drop out. "If you don't want to run, it's all right," he replied, "But I'm afraid you'll be sorry afterward."

"Fanny looked up at him," as eminent sportswriter Ron Fimrite describes, "her distinctive blue-gray eyes streaked with red. She suddenly realized that all her life 'I had wanted to do everything the best.' She would run." Holland's "Magnificent Mama," as she was later called, won that heat in record time, as well as the final, and then anchored the winning 4 x 100-meter relay for a total of four gold medals in five days. Afterwards, she called home over Dutch radio: "Poppa! Dance now around the kitchen table!"

The other memorable Olympic moment of these Games came in the rapid-fire pistol shooting competition. Sergeant

Karoly Takacs of the Hungarian army had been an expert shot and world champion in rapid-fire pistol competition in the late 1930s, but lost his right hand in a grenade explosion. After only a month's recuperation, Takacs stoically began to train again—in secret—by switching hands. Upon his arrival in London he met then world champion and heavily favored Carlos Valiente of Argentina.

"Valiente was very surprised to see me," Takacs told Bud Greenspan in an interview for *The Greatest Moments in Olympic History*. "He thought my career was over. He asked why I was in London. I told him, 'I'm here to learn.' He looked at me quite strange."

Shooting with his left hand, Takacs astonished the assembled crowd by shattering Valiente's world record by ten full points, earning the gold medal. On the victory stand Valiente was the epitome of sportsmanship, shaking hands with his valiant competitor, then suggesting, "Captain Takacs, you have learned quite enough."

In the postwar era, Olympic competition was intensified by the tensions of the Cold War. What was meant to be peaceful competition between talented young athletes began to take on tones of the political antagonisms being played out between East and West. These pressures were reflected in the 1952 Games in Helsinki, which were exceedingly well run but riddled with martial metaphors, as in the statement by Pjotr Sobolev, secretary-general of the Soviet Olympic Committee: "Sports will be a weapon in the fight for peace and the promotion of friendship among all peoples."

As Dave Anderson points out in *The Olympics*, "Now, with the Soviets finally competing in the Olympics, unofficial team points were upstaging individual accomplishments." The unofficial national competition may have garnered a lot of attention at the time, but in history's rearview mirror what we see is a handful of superb competitions, worthy of recollection, between single athletes.

Czech police officer Emil Zátopek and his wife, Dana, became national heroes because of their spirited performances, which came to personify sheer athletic determination. Described by *New York Times* sports columnist Red Smith as "running like a man with a noose around his neck," and by *Sports Illustrated*'s Ron Fimrite as running if he were "enduring the torture of the damned," Zátopek always appeared to be in utter pain and on the verge of collapse, which he claimed was unconscious, though it could have been one of his patented psychological ploys. Aware or not, no one ever *appeared* to run harder or with as much sheer desire, which simultaneously endeared him to spectators and put the fear of the gods into his opponents. His own modest explanation only burnished the legend, "I was not talented enough to run and smile at the same time."

Even with such enormous expectations, Zátopek still managed to pull off one of the most impressive medal sweeps in Olympic history. Early in the competition he won the 10,000-meter race, and then a few days later, he matched that victory with another in the 5,000 meters. As he was leaving the victory stand he noticed his wife striding across the field to take part in the women's javelin competition, and he ran over to show her his gold medal. "Emil, let me have it, I will hold it for good luck."

"On her first throw," writes Greenspan, "Dana broke the Olympic record and her effort held up throughout the competition. The Zátopeks became the first and only married couple ever to win Olympic gold medals on the same day in separate events."

A few days later, Emil stunned the gathering with the news he was going to run the marathon, an event he'd never competed in. When asked why, he said, in jest, "At present, the score of the contest in the Zátopek family is 2–1 [in medals]. The result is too close. To restore some prestige I will try to improve on it—in the marathon race." In truth, he was already bored with the competition and wanted a new challenge. In the grand tradition of heroes like Odysseus, who used both wit and wiles, head and heart, Zátopek upset the favorite, Jim Peters of Great Britain, by keeping pace with him the first half of the race, then slyly asking him, in perfect English, "I have not run in a marathon before. Don't you think we should run a little faster?" The ruse worked. Peters was so disspirited that Zátopek soon sped off and no one could catch him. Years later, he described his winning strategy in the marathon: "I just kept on running and when I entered the stadium the 80,000 people were screaming, 'Zátopek, Zátopek, Zátopek!' and I won my third gold medal in Helsinki."

His bravado was an essential element of his mythic mask. Just as the ancients admired the athletes who knew how to transform "pain into fame," as Pindar wrote, so also are we dazzled to witness modern athletes do the same. Behind Zátopek's mask lurked a secret: the effort took so much out of him he was unable to walk for a week after the marathon. "But," he said, "it was the most pleasant exhaustion I have ever known."

Zátopek's Olympic spirit of sportsmanship and admiration for valiant competition was borne out years later when he was visited by Ron Clarke, the great Australian runner. Clarke had set numerous world records but had never emerged victorious from his Olympic races. When Clark was about to take leave, the Czech champion presented him with a small gift box and told him not to unwrap it until he was on the plane flying home. When he did open it, Clarke was astonished to find an Olympic gold medal and a note that read: "Dear Ron, I have won four gold medals [including a gold medal in the 10,000 meters at London]. It is only right that you should have one of them. Your friend. Emil."

ONE NATION
MARCHING TOGETHER

In 1956, the Games held in Melbourne were disturbed due to boycotts by Egypt, Iraq, and Lebanon because of the Israeli takeover of the Suez Canal, and boycotts by Holland, Spain, and Switzerland because of the Soviet invasion of Hungary. But these losses were partially offset by the first-time inclusion of a combined team from West and East Germany. Once again, the world press obsessed over national point tallies, embittering thousands of athletes and dozens of teams from the nations not involved in the Cold War tensions.

In the Olympic world's equivalent of poetic justice, Australia captured eight golds in its national sport, swimming, while adding another three, won by Betty Cuthbert, in track and field. American Bobby Joe Morrow earned three racing golds, in the 100 meters and 200 meters. Morrow's training regimen included eleven hours of sleep a night, which ensured him the chance to compete with preternatural calm. "Whatever success I have had," he said, "is due to being so perfectly relaxed that I can feel my jaw muscles wiggle."

But the big story was that of a twenty-two-year-old sailor from New Jersey, Milt Campbell, who had trained for the hurdles but did not qualify. "I was stunned," he said. "But then God seemed to reach into my heart and tell me he didn't want me to compete in the hurdles, but in the decathlon."

With Olympian graciousness, Campbell credits one of his opponents with pushing him to his limits. During the grueling 1,500-meter run, Campbell says, he heard one of the other competitors urging him to run harder, to go for the Olympic record.

"I looked and saw that it was Ian Bruce of Australia, who wasn't even in the top ten. And he kept yelling at me . . . come on boy . . . you can do it.' So he started to sprint and I started to sprint with him. I couldn't believe it. Here's a guy whom I never met urging me on... Incredibly we passed the Russian [Kuznyetsov] and now Bruce and I were racing to the finish. At the line he just nipped me out... but I'll never forget him."

Even though he came in second, Campbell's time of 4:50:6 earned him the Olympic decathalon record. "They can talk about the true Olympic spirit and laugh at it," he later said, "but Ian Bruce showed me it does exist."

A bold innovation for the closing ceremonies at Melbourne that became a model for future Games was suggested by John Ian Wing, a seventeen-year-old Australian-Chinese boy, in a letter addressed to Sir Wildfred Kent Hughes of the Melbourne Olympic Organizing Committee:

> Dear Friends:
>
> I am a Chinese boy and have just turned seventeen years of age. Before the Games I thought everything would be in a muddle. However, I am quite wrong. It is the most successful Games ever staged... Mr. Hughes, I believe it has been suggested a march be put on during the closing ceremonies and you said it couldn't be done. I think it can be done... The march I have in mind is different than the one during the Opening Ceremony... During the march there will be only one nation... what more could anybody want if the whole world could be made as one nation?
>
> John Ian Wing

Later, Shirley Strickland, Australian medalist in three Olympics, described her feelings about marching with chosen friends from different countries around the world rather than filing in as separate national teams. "The intermingling of athletes in the parade typified the brotherhood of sport which the Olympic Games had developed. The flame died, the athletes departed, but the spirit and harmony of this Olympiad will stay with us for the rest of our lives."

Four years later, Rome finally hosted its first Olympics. Originally scheduled for 1908 but postponed due to the eruption of Vesuvius, they were flamboyantly staged in 1960 with the ancient Roman ruins as a backdrop. Gymnasium events were held in the Baths of Caracalla, wrestlers tussled in the Basilica of Maxentius, and the marathon, which was won by the barefoot Ethiopian Abebe Bikila, wound from Capitoline Hill, along the torch-lit Appian Way, to the Arch of Constantine. After the race, Bikila attempted to demystify his accomplishment by saying, "I could have gone around the course again without any difficulty."

Two athletes at these Games stood out as the latest to embody the Olympic ideals of perseverance and courage in surmounting a tremendous challenge. The timeless human fascination with overcoming hard times was summed up by Doc Young, an African-American journalist, in the documentary film *Stride for Glory:* "Nothing develops a sports champion more than a hard way to go." Talent and technique are admirable, but as Susan Wels writes, it is "the beauty of the human form and the struggle and grace of competition that form the emotional heart of the art of the Games."

Wilma Rudolph, born in rural Tennessee, had suffered from pneumonia and scarlet fever as a little girl. These afflictions left her crippled and subject to braces and painful daily leg rubs by parents, brothers, and sisters until she was twelve. "My mother taught me very early to believe that I could achieve anything I wanted to. The first was to learn to walk without braces." She learned to do more than that. By age sixteen she had become a star basketball player and runner and had qualified for the U.S. team at the Melbourne Games. But it was the Roman Games, where she was affectionately called *la Gazzella Nera*, "the Black

Gazelle," that made her an international favorite, and not only for her inborn talents. The day before her first race she tripped on a drainpipe while training and severely sprained her ankle. On race day she heavily taped the ankle and ran through the wall of pain anyway, tying the world record in the 100 meters. Later she also won the 200-meter race and ran the last leg of the four-person 100-meter relay.

Near the finish line of one of her races, someone asked a French photographer who had come in first. "Who won? *La Gazella, naturellement. La Chattanooga choo-choo.*"

Wilma Rudolph, winner of two gold medals at the 1960 Rome Olympics.

Her Olympic courage endeared her to the world, as did her sense of humor and selflessness. When asked how she got to be so fast, she replied: "I am number seventeen out of nineteen children. I had to be fast to get anything to eat." When asked what was the most important moment in her Olympic experience, she said, "Oh, without question it was the relay. For then I could stand on the podium with my Tigerbelle teammates whom I love . . . and we could celebrate together."

The Roman Games also saw the spectacular rise of a young light-heavyweight boxer, the "Louisville Lip," Cassius Clay, who dazzled the media with wit, poetry, and sheer ebullience as much as he dazzled his fellow boxers with his footwork and punches. Winning the gold, Clay was the very embodiment of the *enthusiasm* that, according to the ancients, revealed the "god within," or at least the blessing of the gods. His utter joy before and after his bouts was in dramatic contrast to his fiery demeanor in the ring, where he demolished opponents.

The glory that once was Rome, however, did not hold up at home. To his searing disappointment, Clay quickly realized that nothing had changed for him in the States. As Wallechinsky tells the story, "An owner of a Louisville restaurant refused to serve Clay because he was African-American. Afterwards, a motorcycle gang chased Clay and a friend and a fight ensued. Within four years, he was so disillusioned, he threw his once-cherished gold medal off a bridge into the Ohio River, changed his name to Muhammad Ali, became a conscientious objector, and won the heavyweight title three different times. In his autobiography, he wrote, 'I wanted something that meant more than that. Something that was as proud of me as I would be of it.'"

Who would have thought, asked novelist Norman Mailer in a recent documentary about Ali, that this brash boxer would go on to become arguably the most recognizable face in the world?

It happened, Mailer said, because no one ever brought so much *joy* to the world of sports." Indeed, as Ali fused the arts of ballet and boxing, poetry and sport, he evoked memories of W. B. Yeats's immortal poem:

> O body swayed to music,
> O brightening glance,
> How can we know the dancer
> From the dance?

On a lighter note, vaulter Don Bragg fulfilled a lifelong dream by auditioning before the world for the role of Tarzan while standing on the victory stand. Cupping his hands like Johnny Weismuller and the others who had gone before him, Bragg bellowed like the beloved ape man, and the international crowd roared with recognition.

Later, he got the job.

THE HAPPY GAMES

The first Olympic Games ever to be staged in Asia had been scheduled for Tokyo in 1940, but Japan's invasion of China led to their cancellation. Nineteen years later, Tokyo made another bid for the Games and won over those by Detroit, Brussels, and Vienna. The award was considered a conciliatory gesture by the Olympic organization that acknowledged Japan's acceptance back into the international community.

The 1964 Games in Tokyo began on a somberly moving note when the Olympic torch was carried into the stadium by nineteen-year-old Oshinoro Sakai, born outside of Hiroshima on August 6, 1945. The significance of the choice for torchbearer was lost on no one; Sakai had been born an hour before the first atomic bomb was dropped over that city. The Eighteenth Olympiad signified both the rebirth of Japan and the Olympics' contribution to countering martial competition with peaceful competition.

The civility and hospitality of the Japanese was offset by some ominous developments, including the first known appearance of performance-enhancing anabolic steroids, and even the first two shoe contracts. There were also sterling examples of athletes carrying the torch of inspiration. Heavyweight boxer Joe Frazier somehow ignored the agonizing pain of a broken hand to defeat German Hans Huber. Barefoot marathon winner from the Rome Games, Ethiopian Abebe Bikila, ran with shoes this time but also had to overcome the pain of a recent appendectomy to win his second consecutive title. In swimming, Australian Dawn Fraser seized the 100-meter freestyle title despite debilitating pain from neck injuries sustained in a recent car crash. The flamboyant Fraser etched her name into the Olympic halls of infamy when she was banned from international competition for ten years for stealing a flag from the Imperial grounds. She insisted the whole thing was an innocent prank performed while irrepressibly celebrating her Olympic victory.

For American discus thrower Al Oerter, the Tokyo Games were his chance to win a third consecutive crown. But during a practice session the week before the Games, he ripped some cartilage in his rib cage. Oerter took ice treatments, aspirin, and Novocaine, and still he was in agony. "But these are the Olympics," he recalled later, "and you die before you don't compete in the Olympics." Compete he did, "wrapped up in bandages like a mummy" and swallowing capsules of ammonia so he could think straight. On his fifth and last throw, he broke the Olympic record and won his third straight (of four) discus titles—and the admiration of the entire sporting world for his ability to play through the pain.

But perhaps the most luminous Olympic moment flashed in the 15,000-meter race, which was graced by one of the most glorious fields of runners in racing history. World-record holder Australian Ron Clarke and Tunisian Mohammed Gammoudi were the two heavy favorites, while Native American runner Billy Mills went virtually ignored. As expected, Clarke led at the halfway mark, but with one lap to go Mills was running even with him, with Gammoudi a few cluttered feet behind. Suddenly Clarke got stuck behind a straggler and was boxed in by the upstart Mills. The Australian tried to coax him to move, then nudged him, exiling Mills to the outside lane for a moment—but then Gammoudi pushed past both of them and into the lead.

At the last curve, Mills was in a fiercely congested fourth place. For the briefest of moments, he said later, he thought of quitting; then he remembered he had made a commitment and there was really no way he could quit. That is when he heard an inner voice telling him he still had a chance.

With only fifteen yards to go, Mills made his miraculous move and came flying out of the spidery pack of flailing arms and legs, running with a kick whose suddenness and ferocity stunned everyone in the Olympic stadium. As he ran, he kept whispering to himself, "I can win, I can win, I can win"—and he sprinted past Clarke and Gammoudi, who later said they had never even heard of him. The photograph of Mills crossing the finish line with his hands thrust triumphantly into the sky is one of the most jubilant images ever taken of an athlete.

His startling victory was called "the greatest display of pressure running I have ever seen by an American" by Avery Brundage, head of the International Olympic Committee. Not only did Mills break his own personal best time by an astonishing 46 seconds, he smashed the Olympic record by nearly 8 seconds. "I can't believe it," he said after the race. "I suppose I was the only person who thought I had a chance."

Revealing the courageous heart of a true champion,
Billy Mills outsprints his rivals to win the 10,000-
meter race at the 1964 Tokyo Games.

"Ironically," writes Nicholas Sparks, Mills's biographer, "an official approached him after the race and asked the question, 'Who are you?' Bill had been running in search of that answer his whole life, and now, for the first time, he finally knew the answer."

When asked later what had run through his mind during his exuberant moments on the victory stand, Mills said he wished he had had an eagle feather to go along with the American flag he was holding. Then he added that he had looked around the stadium and seen the running track as "the great circle of being," an astonishing reference to the Sioux image of the sacred hoop of creation. This means that during his moment of triumph, his thoughts turned away from personal accomplishment to what his victory might mean to his people, who believed that the great circle had been broken but would someday be healed.

Off the track, Mills continues to "walk his talk," as Native Americans say, by devoting his life to his "Running Strong" organization and mentoring Indian youth, encouraging them to believe that the true champions are the ones who follow their dreams with dignity and pride. "At a given place," he tells audiences, "on a given day at a given time—something magical can happen. This is a belief shared by every athlete during the Parade of Nations at the Opening Ceremonies of the Olympic Games."

Mills's blazing moment of glory was the fruit of his steadfast training and stouthearted dedication; his commitment to passing on the torch of inspiration reveals his gift for embodying a balance between the ancient Greek ideal of a healthy mind in a healthy body and the American Indian ideal of tending to the fire in the soul of your nation's young people.

The 1968 Mexico City Games opened a few days after the brutal slaying of hundreds of students by government troops in Mexico City's town square. This tragic beginning set the stage for the infamous Black Power protests by 100-meter winner Tommy Smith and silver-medal winner John Carlos, and for the introduction of sex tests for women athletes (first used at the 1968 Grenoble Winter Games). Yet beyond the grim political and social realities at this Olympiad there were a startling number of spectacular performances. Thirty-four world records and thirty-eight Olympic records were set in Mexico City's mile-high altitude. Fleet-footed American Lee Evans broke the world record in the 400 meters, Al Oerter won his third straight gold medal in the discus, and another Yank, Jim Hines, shattered the equivalent of the four-minute mile barrier in the sprints by breaking ten seconds in the 100-meter race.

In the marathon, Abebe Bikila attempted to win his third straight title but left with an injury, and the gold went to his teammate Mamo Wolde. However, the world's attention centered upon a bloodied and heavily bandaged figure who stumbled into the Olympic stadium an hour after the other runners, "the last man in the marathon." His effort was described by one sportswriter: "Today we have seen a young African runner who symbolizes the finest in the human spirit . . . a performance that gives true meaning to sport . . . a performance that lifts sport out of the category of grown men playing games . . . a performance that gives meaning to the word courage . . . All honor to John Stephen Akhwari of Tanzania."

The visual impact of Akhwari's effort was impressive enough, but it was his eloquent response to reporters' questions about *why* he wanted to finish that truly cemented his legend. "Why endure it?" he asked rhetorically. "I don't think you understand. My country did not send me to Mexico City to start the race. They sent me to finish the race."

Of all the records that were set during the Mexico City Games, the one best remembered is the "leap into the twenty-first century," the record-annihilating long jump by Bob Beamon.

On his first leap from the jumping board, Beamon elevated nearly six feet as he flew through the air with his arms and legs stretched out like a prehistoric bird. He landed with such force at the end of sand pit—and beyond the measuring marker—that he bounced outside the pit. While someone searched out an old steel measuring tape, it became obvious to the other jumpers that he had set a world record.

"Compared to this jump," sighed the Soviet athlete Igor Terovanesyan, "we are children." Welsh jumper Lynn Davies

© IOC/Olympic Museum Collections

Winner of the first Olympic Spirit Award at the 1968 Mexico City Games, Bob Beamon shattered the world long-jump record by almost two feet.

told Beamon, "You have destroyed this event." Sprinter Ron Freeman murmured to himself across the field "Hope he didn't foul on *that* one." Beamon's American teammate and former record holder, Ralph Boston, calmly said to him, "Bob, I think it's over 29 feet." Beamon replied, "What happened to 28 feet?"

In Billy Mills's words: "On any given day . . ."

On this day Beamon had somehow accessed the primal power of the Olympics—the possibility of the impossible. In an event where records were broken by quarter-inches and half-inches at a time, he had smashed the world record by *twenty-two inches* and won the gold medal by nearly-two-and-a-half feet. He was so stunned, he collapsed on the infield, suffering from a cataleptic seizure. Later he would say he was overcome by pure joy and tears of happiness.

The 1968 Games saw another kind of psychological barrier broken, but in a surprising and, to many, humorous way. Until Dick Fosbury came along, the high jump was a conservative event in which athletes leapt over the bar like a pair of slashing scissors, head forward, followed by a roll over the bar and then the legs. This wasn't good enough for Fosbury, who had his sights on both world and Olympic records. His early attempts at innovation met with mockery, but he learned to follow his heart, which meant going over the bar *backwards* in what is now universally called "the Fosbury Flop."

"I began to trust my instincts when it came to jumping," he said. "Within each of us lies a form, a talent, or a gift that we can develop if we just pay attention." Even if it sometimes means turning things upside down.

In Mexico City, Fosbury says, his early leaps were followed by exclamations about the *loco Americano,* but with each successful jump the cheers grew louder. Finally, the bar was set at 7 feet, 4¼ inches. The immense stadium grew quiet when he missed his first two attempts.

"The quiet was eerie," he later told John Naber. "But I was totally focused and took nearly all my full two minutes. I ran at the bar, threw my body into the air and watched as the bar glided beneath me. Looking up from the pit, I saw it was clean. The crowd erupted in *Ole's!* and I bounced out of the pit." Fosbury had set new American and Olympic records with his unique technique. He continues to draw life lessons from that gold-winning effort.

"To awaken the Olympian within," he says, "we have to look at what works now, not just what worked in the past . . . That's how you make a winner out of a 'flop.'"

The Germans hoped that the brotherhood and beauty of the 1972 Munich Games would erase memories of the tensions that had accompanied the 1936 Berlin Games. These hopes were shattered when Palestinian terrorists kidnapped eleven members of the Israeli team, held them hostage in the Olympic Village, and then executed them during the attempted getaway.

Nevertheless, the IOC decided, the Games must go on. German president Gustav Heinemann spoke to the horrific violation of the Olympic sanctuary and evoked the ancient spirit of Olympia when he appealed to every country "to overcome hatred" and "to pave the way for reconciliation."

In the hope that the contests would prove a healing balm for the heartbreak, and after a grieving period of less than twenty-four hours, the competitions resumed. By then many entire teams, including those from Israel, Norway, the Netherlands, Egypt, Syria, Kuwait, and the Philippines, had lost heart and returned home.

Among the athletes who stayed the course was twenty-two-year-old American swimmer and dental student Mark Spitz, who "swam his brains out" en route to breaking seven world records and winning seven gold medals. But as grand as the personal accomplishment was, he felt the touch of the Olympic spirit when his teammates honored him after his last victory by lifting him on their shoulders. The triumphant moment was memorialized in a famous photograph. "That picture with my teammates," Spitz later said, "holding me high above them I enjoy more than the one that was taken with the seven gold medals around my neck. Having a tribute from your teammates is a feeling that can never be duplicated."

Sixteen-year-old Ulrike Meyfarth of Germany became the youngest gold medalist in an individual track and field event when she leapt 6 feet, 3½ inches in the women's high jump. Crowd favorite Kip Keino, from Kenya, took first place in the

3,000-meter steeplechase, ahead of his teammate Benjamin Jipcho and Tapio Kantanen of Finland.

But it was Olga Korbut, the "Munchkin from Munich," a four-foot-eleven-inch, seventeen-year-old gymnast from Grodno, in Byelorussia, who has come to personify the Olympic spirit of those Games. Her courageous recovery from a humiliating mistake on the uneven bars changed the face of the Games and her sport. As the eyes of the world watched her on television Korbut competed with a flair that transcended technique. With a radiant smile that was in dramatic contrast to years of glum expressions and joyless performances by Eastern European athletes, she not only masked her disappointment, but she also won gold medals in the balance beam and floor exercises—and the hearts of Olympic fans around the world. And like Dorando Pietri's popularizing of the marathon, tens of thousands of young girls wanted to emulate her. Enrollment in women's gymnastics programs exploded over the next few years.

Afterwards, Korbut was taken ceremoniously to the White House, where she met President Nixon. He confided to the elfin athlete a few words that harkened back to the Olympics' original spirit and the true joy of sports. "He told me," she said, "that my performance in Munich did more for reducing the political tension during the Cold War between our two countries than the embassies were able to do in five years."

The Munich Games were immortalized in another way in the stirring documentary film, *Visions of Eight*—actually a collection of eight short films by different international filmmakers. In the sequence entitled "The Losers," French filmmaker Claude Lelouch created a deeply moving montage of those who had *not* emerged victorious from their competition. He was intrigued with how highly competitive athletes deal with the inevitability of loss. "At some point everyone must learn to live with defeat," he wrote. "I wanted to see how each person accepts that fact, how losers meet sudden loneliness."

The Montreal Games, in 1976, were staged with great expectations. Mayor Jean Drapeau vowed, "It is time to bring back the real truth of the Olympics. These will be modest, self-financed Games." Instead, they proved to be a financial nightmare for the city and the province. The Games were also riddled with boycotts by African athletes protesting New Zealand's participation, because it had recently played South Africa in a rugby match, and plagued with mass disqualifications for athletes who tested positive for steroids.

The competition was highlighted by the phenomenal "double-double" achievement of Lasse Viren of Finland, who won both the 5,000- and 10,000-meter runs for the second consecutive Olympiad. American Bruce Jenner won the decathlon, an accomplishment marked by his remarkable achievement of eight personal bests in ten events.

"I started to feel there was nothing I couldn't do if I had to," he said at the time. "It was a feeling of awesome power, except that I was in awe of myself . . . I was rising above myself, doing things I had no right doing."

The Montreal Games were "perfect" in at least one aspect, the woman's gymnastic competition. It was there that the undisputed star of the Games emerged. The daughter of a Romanian mechanic, the enchanting fourteen-year-old Nadia Comaneci became an instant star on television screens around the world. Her uneven bar performance in the team competition defied history and technology simultaneously. She became the first gymnast to earn a "10," which is perfection, an achievement considered so unlikely that scoreboards are not made to flash double-digit scores. After Comaneci's dazzling performance only a lonely "1" went up on the board, leave the extra "0" to the audience's imagination. Confusion reigned until the arena announcer declared her score to the astonished spectators.

Of her breathtaking performance she later said, "I knew my routine was flawless. I had performed it many times before in practice the same way." Her courage and excellence led to six more perfect scores for a total of seven, and a final tally of three gold, one silver, and one bronze medal.

"Her precision and daring in gymnastics have never been seen before in an Olympics," wrote Frank Deford in *Sports Illustrated.* "And few heroines in any sport ever so captivated the Games. She was perfectly cast for the moment, bursting upon the world with the first perfect Olympic gymnastic score, a 10.0, on the first day of competition, thereby dramatically ridding Montreal of much of the rancor and turmoil of international politics. She was brilliant and beguiling, and because of her youth a great sense of hope and history was instantly attached to her. There was at once the chance to see greatness. For the rare privilege of witnessing the birth of a legend, people splurged $100 on a $16 seat." Years later, she was asked about the true spirit of sport and said: "Never pray for an easy life. Pray to be a strong person."

American John Naber became the first backstroke swimmer to crack the two-minute barrier while winning the gold medal in the 200-meter race. He collected two more gold medals in relay races and a silver medal in the 200-meter freestyle. Naber went on to become a broadcaster at six subsequent Olympics and president of the U.S. Olympians. He is also a tireless speaker on the inspirational circuit, where his aim is to help people in both sports and the business world "awaken the Olympian within."

"*Citius, altius, fortius* means *swifter, higher, stronger,* not swiftest, highest, strongest," Naber writes. "It is the desire for improvement—the pursuit of greatness that makes better *people* of the athletes who compete for their countries."

In the great tradition of passing the torch of inspiration, Naber encourages other athletes to share their stories and become ambassadors of "the timeless truths" of the Games. By passing along their knowledge and their spirit, "great Olympic motivators teach us how to overcome obstacles, how to focus our attention on matters of importance, how to eliminate negative thinking, how innovations and creative thought *do* make a difference, how to attend to details and how to work hard."

The 1980 Moscow Summer Games were stigmatized by the Jimmy Carter–led boycott in response to the Soviet invasion of Afghanistan. Some governments allowed their athletes to compete on their own initiative, but the Games were marked by strange security precautions, the Soviet fans' poor sportsmanship, and questionable judging by Russian judges.

One beacon of light was Daley Thompson, from Great Britain, who won his first decathlon crown. In an interview in 1984, he described his passion for the ancient ten-event competition as rooted in the political value of the Games and the importance of competing against yourself:

> Everything at the end of the day is a test, and the Olympic philosophy is to enter the arena, make your effort, and do your best. It is one of those utopian ideals, which I don't believe should be lost on the world. It may not be possible for them to actually occur, but there's nothing wrong with trying to strive for what they set out for—and that is that the youth of the world should get together and have a good time and maybe when they're older and in charge of countries and companies a bit of [the Olympic experience] will rub off and we'll all be nicer together. I don't believe that ideal is out of place. I always try and strive for the best for myself, and in that aspect I'm probably out of date. But perhaps we need a few more like me!

CHAPTER V

THE FIERY PURSUIT OF EXCELLENCE

1980–2000

Why should you push yourself? The answer: Because the rewards of reaching *for excellence truly are profound. I'm not talking about a pay raise, a plaque or even a gold medal. It's* living into a purpose or a calling *that enlivens even the most mundane tasks. It's a deep pride in the life we are living.*

—NANCY HOGSHEAD,
gold-medal winner,
1984 Los Angeles

By honing [as if on a whetstone] someone born
for excellence a man may, with divine help
urge him on to prodigious fame.

—PINDAR,
Tenth Olympian Ode

And in the tenth year of his wandering, which itself followed ten years of war before the walls of Troy, the weary but crafty "man of many turns," Odysseus of Ithaca, washed ashore on the island of Scheria, home of the famous shipbuilders, the Phaecians. The king's lovely daughter, Nausicaa, was playing ball with her maids when she discovered Odysseus on the beach, and she brought him to her father's court. In the spirit of the times, the stranger was treated with consummate hospitality. King Alcinous promised him one of his finest ships to speed his passage home, commanded a feast for him, and asked the herald to summon Demodokos, the blind bard, to entertain him with songs. The poet, "beloved above all others by the Muse," strummed his lyre and sang about the deeds of Odysseus himself during the Trojan War. Odysseus listened and wept when he heard the names of his lost friends, yet none around him knew why he grieved, since he had not revealed his identity.

Once the singing and feasting were over, the king told those assembled in the royal hall, "Let us go out and divert ourselves with various athletic contests so that when our guest goes home he will tell his friends how we surpass others in boxing and wrestling and jumping and footracing."

Then the king led the way to the stadium, where the courtiers watched the young men of the island race, wrestle, jump, box, and hurl the discus. But Odysseus was distracted, for his heart was full of thoughts of home. The king's son, Laodamus, felt moved by the stranger's loneliness. Just as today a young lad on a football pitch in England, or a teenage girl basketball player in Vernon, Ontario, or a twenty-something hockey player in Wausau, Wisconsin, might invite the new kid in town to kick a ball around, play some hoops, or chase a hockey puck, the prince invited Odysseus to play with them in these now-famous words: "Won't you too, sir, try your hand at some contest, that is, if you know any. You have the look of an athlete to me. There is no greater fame for a man than that which he wins with his footwork or the skill of his hands. Have a try now and put away your cares. Your journey home is near at hand, and we have already prepared for you a ship and crew."

At first Odysseus waved them away, saying his heart was heavy with grief and he was thinking more about getting home than about playing games. His refusal was mistaken as a sign of fear or cowardice by Euryalos, who was still full of himself after winning the wrestling match. The foolhardy youth uttered what would have been fighting words anywhere in ancient Greece, and still are in most of the world today: "You're no athlete."

Infuriated, Odysseus replied that the wrestler was proof that the gods never grant one person all the gifts. "Take yourself, for example," he thundered, "a masterpiece in body which not even a god could improve, but empty in the head. Your sneering made my heart beat faster. I am no ninny at sports, as you would have it. Indeed I think I was among the best in my time, but now I exist in pain and misery, having risked and endured so much in the wars of men and the toils of the sea. Yet despite the ravages of these evil things I will try your tests of strength."

Odysseus seized the discus, and, as Homer vividly describes, "whirling, he hurled it from his mighty hand, and the stone whistled through the air . . . soared so freely from the hero's hand that it overpassed the marks of every other."

Mysteriously now, the wise goddess Athena appeared disguised as a judge who marked the distance and said to him, "Even a blind man, sir, could judge your throw by feeling for it; it is not mixed in with the others, but far out in front. You may take heart from this contest, for no Phaecian will come close, much less beat you."

His heavy heart lightened by his prodigious effort, Odysseus told the crowd, "You have worked me up to such a pitch that I shall not flinch from anything." His passion was such that none dared move, none dared utter a word. Instead, they waited for their king to speak for them.

Alcinous then declared, "Sir, what you have said to us is not unwelcome, for it is natural that you should want to show your *arete,* since you were angered by that man standing up in the gathering and sneering at you as if at your *arete*, although no man in his right senses would do so."

The wise king beseeched the hero to remember them kindly and called for another celebration. "But come," he said to everyone present, "let us have the best dancers of the Phaecians dance before us, so that when our guest goes home he will tell his friends how we surpass others in seamanship and running and dancing and singing."

THE EXCELLENT LIFE

This glorious account of what has been called Homeric athletics is like a stained-glass window on which we can see portrayed the many-colored splendor of ancient sports. It is in the *Odyssey* and the *Iliad* that we first discover the deep spirit of sports, the desire to race, wrestle, throw, and box—not for money, nor for prizes, but for the challenge of the contest and the rapture that comes from doing well.

Looking further through the glass, we can also recognize the root behavior of our own desire to occasionally "show our *arete*," our excellence, to the world, especially when challenged. As Joseph Campbell once said to me, the "miracle of the myths" is the way we often perceive ourselves in them, how they show us reflections of "our own inward life." The scene on the island of Scheria is startlingly familiar because the sparks of competitive fire, flashes of pride, and impassioned displays of grace and skill can be found today in stadiums the world over.

Pericles, in one of the famous speeches he delivered as leader of Athens, said, "And we have not forgotten to provide for our weary spirits many relaxations from toil; we have regular games and sacrifices throughout the year; at home our life is refined; and the delight which we daily feel in all these things helps us to banish melancholy." These inexhaustibly intriguing lines suggest one of the transcendent functions of sports, the *uplifting* of our *down*trodden lives.

Historian William J. Baker speculates, in *Sports in the Western World*, on the universality of the competitive impulse: "Human beings cannot live by bread alone. They dream and they strive. Not merely for warmth do they take fire from the altar of the gods; curiosity is their glory and their pain. They climb mountains, cross uncharted seas, and explore outer space for reasons other than material benefit. They thrive on challenges.

Seekers of laurels, they especially measure themselves in competition with fellow humans. Where there is no contest, they create one. From deep within, and from millennia past, comes the impulse for athletic competition . . . Little wonder that competitive sport thrives most in societies where achievement rather than mere birth is the means to success and acclaim."

Bernd Heinrich agrees that this urge is tens of thousands of years old. He has spent his life trying to find a link between the innate urge to run as expressed in ancient rock art and the drive to run *hard*, to train right through the pain, as expressed by his fellow long distance runners. "There is nothing quite so gentle, deep, and irrational as our running—and nothing quite so savage, and so wild," he writes. "For me, the Bushman painting [of ancient runners] embodies the connection between running, hunting, and humanity's striving toward excellence."

The transcendent dimension of sports has long fascinated author, lecturer, and long distance runner Michael Murphy, who has spent the last five decades rigorously documenting the extraordinary parallels between athletic and religious discipline. In his book about the mystical side of sports, with Rhea White, *In the Zone*, he comments, "This willingness to suffer so much for sport can be understood as a concentrated expression of our drive to express a deeper perfection and beauty we secretly sense. That deeper perfection is more important to many athletes than prizes or applause." This drive, Murphy believes, reflects our desire for self-transcendence, which plays an active role in the evolution of the species. For him, "Sports are our very own 'Western yoga,' a vehicle for lifting the common life to divine heights." And the feeling or sensation of this lifting, this elevation, has become known as *flow*, the state of being *in it*, in rhythm, in synch, *in the zone*.

Dan Millman, a former world-class trampoline champion and Hall of Fame gymnast, is also fascinated with the vision and dedication of athletes who aspire to utmost excellence in their field. The persistent question of *how* they reach it inspired him to write several strong books on the topic, including *The Inner Athlete*. "Athletes who achieve one-pointed attention," he observes, "feel totally 'on,' completely present. That state has been called 'flow,' it has also been called 'the zone.' But whatever we call it, the inner athlete calls it 'home.'"

"Flow state" is a way of describing effortless excellence. It makes us feel like we are back in our body, that we are, if even for a moment, whole. This flow isn't accidental or mere luck; it is the fruit of practice, clarity of purpose, intense devotion, and focus. Basketball superstar Michael Jordan has referred to this heightened state as the reward for years of hard work, focus, and preparation. When it happens, it "provides a glimpse of perfection," in the words of researcher Mihaly Csikszentmihalyi. It is the result of excellence and has little to do with medals, trophies, or fame. It is inner gold. It is the marvel of marvels. It is the perfect moment when everything comes together. As the ancient Greeks used to say, it is the instant when Aphrodite—goddess of beauty, mother of Eros, love itself, and grandmother of Joy—smiles her blessing upon the world, including its athletes. This is why beauty, strength and pleasure—the erotics of sports—have always been inseparable qualities at the elite level. Which is to say, flow cannot be seized and it cannot be faked. Like love, it must be earned; like grace, it can only be granted; like inspiration, it arrives only after excellent inner work. And nothing great can be achieved without it.

In the larger game of life, the feeling of flow resembles the feeling of coming home again, which is why the search for excellence is no ordinary journey but an odyssey. Short journeys teach us nothing, say the poets and the committed athletes; long journeys teach us what we can use when we get home. The meandering journey to excellence, the excellent athletes tell us, is a chance to "raise your game to another level," an opportunity to improve, to learn how to deal with defeat and how to work and play with others as a team.

Michael Jordan, considered the standard bearer of excellence in basketball, led the Dream Team in the 1992 Games in Barcelona.

The white heat of desire that drives that journey reveals the existential dimension of sports, the deeply felt belief that the only meaning is in the *moment*, so it had better be lived—or played—to your utmost. Michael Jordan often claimed that he lived for the chance to see what would happen on the court, what moves he would flash, what "jukes" he would come up with, and he obviously loved surprising even himself. "Each time I step on the basketball court," he said, "I never know what will happen. I live for the moment. I play for the moment."

Another famous passage illuminating the existential side of sports comes from Yuri Vlasov, former world champion Russian weightlifter, poet, and philosopher: "At the peak of tremendous and victorious effort, while the blood is pounding in your head, all suddenly becomes quiet within you. Everything seems clearer and whiter than before, as if great spotlights had been turned on. At that moment you have the conviction that you contain all the power in the world, that you are capable of everything, that you have wings. There is no more precious moment in life than this, the white moment, and you will work very hard for years just to taste it again."

From Odysseus in ancient Greece to Wilma Rudolph in modern Italy, athletes play, compete, and strive to excel even when—even *because*—their hearts are breaking from home-sickness or their spirits are near to shattering from social injus-tice or physical agony. What artists, mystics, and athletes demonstrate is that we can transform suffering into satisfac-tion, pain into joy, through an excellent *effort*. That is what quickens our spirit.

The life-enhancing power of sports, especially in the face of tragedy, has been borne out again and again through his-tory, from the funeral games held in honor of Patroclus in the *Iliad*, to the baseball games played on Sunday afternoons dur-ing the Civil War, to the soccer games between British and German soldiers on Christmas Day, 1917, during World War I. This is why the *cri de coeur* arose from the citizens of New York City in the days after the terrorist attacks of September 11, 2001, for Sarah Hughes to recreate her inspiring, gold-medal-winning skating routine at Rockefeller Center. These cries arise from the cultural soul so that we can say, along with bard Van Morrison, "the healing has begun."

We play on for reasons that transcend escapism. We play on to bring ourselves back to life, to re-create ourselves, to remind ourselves that we have the capacity to be more than ordinary, that we have the courage to be extraordinary, if only for a few moments on the field, in the arena, around the track. We play on to rekindle the fire that is perennially in danger of going out.

To this effect, many ancient people had fire ceremonies, and several, such as the Inca, Maya, and Hopi, had fire races in honor of their gods. The ancient Greeks performed regular torch races to honor Prometheus, the god whose name means "forethought" for having the vision and courage to steal fire from Zeus and give it to human beings, whose sacred duty it is to keep the fire blazing. Pausanius writes: "There is an altar of Prometheus in the Academy [in Athens] and they run from this to the city holding burning torches. The contest is to run and keep the torch burning at the same time. The torch and the victory are extinguished together for the front runner, and the victory passes on to the second-place runner. But if his torch goes out, the third-place winner takes the victory; and if everybody's torches go out, nobody wins."

The Olympic lesson surviving to this day is that winning is not necessarily victory; the laurel is not equivalent to the torch. The true spirit of sports is the fire in our hearts—symbolically, the torch that *each one* in the race, the match, the game, the contest carries. If that fire, that torch, goes out—is smothered, stifled, or crushed—then *nobody wins*.

THE GREEK FIRE

"The inner fire is the most important thing mankind possesses," writes Danish poet Edith Södergran, a conviction shared by Mary Lou Retton, 1984 gold-medal-winning gymnast, who said after her victory, "Each of us has a fire in our hearts for something. It's our goal in life to find it and keep it lit." In Nikos Kazantzakis's incandescent novel *Zorba the Greek*, the irrepressible hero shouts out to the mountain winds that batter his island home of Crete, "You won't put my fire out!" In the book's closing words, the English schoolteacher-narrator describes the literally *inspiring* effect Zorba's fire had on him: "My life with Zorba had enlarged my heart; some of his words had calmed my soul. This man with infallible instinct . . . without losing his breath, had reached the peak of effort and had even gone further."

What Kazantzakis refers to as "the Greek fire" is portrayed in Odysseus as a slow burn that gradually reveals his true character. His honor has been questioned, his manhood is in doubt; he is in danger of losing face, his very identity as a Greek warrior and champion athlete has been challenged. His response is first with a fury of words, then with a superb display of skill. He defends his honor, momentarily banishing his melancholy.

An unexpected insight into the Greek soul comes in the king's remark that Odysseus's desire to reveal his *arete*—his excellence, virtue, skill, pride, valor—is normal. "For it is natural," the king tells him, "to show your *arete*." It is not vainglorious, elitist, or a mere byproduct of male testosterone, but natural and admirable.

By mentioning Odysseus's *arete*, the king acknowledges his guest to be a man of honor and integrity. Moreover, an astonishing detail of the story reveals the king to be on intimate terms with the quality. His wife's name is Arete.

The king's next words reveal his desire that the Phaecians be known as people who excel not only at the helm of a ship and in the stadium but also on the stage—in other words, in mind, body, and soul. This vision reflects the Greek insistence, expressed again and again throughout classical times, that they were not "barbarians" but a civilized people. And what made them civilized in their own eyes in everything they attempted—from the worship of their gods to their art and architecture to their military prowess and athletic skill—was their striving for excellence

The Greek ideal, handed down to us in the phrase "a healthy mind in a healthy body," is illustrated beautifully in this scene. And it is not just talked about, it is *acted* upon, which is the very definition of drama. Odysseus *takes action* and thereby defines himself. Not only does he display outstanding athletic ability, but he does so as a man of spirit, heart, pride, and courage, which is why he is referred to as "that man of wisdom" in the opening lines of the *Odyssey*. This is no ordinary hero. Throughout his story, he does not want to *get away*, which is the hallmark of so many other stories, but wishes above all else to *get back*. The fabulous tales that describe his efforts were called the *nostoi*, "the returns home," which when joined to *algos* or "pain" gave rise in the eighteenth century to the word *nostalgia*, "painful homesickness."

Odysseus has to *earn* his way back home. The "crafty one" must prove himself again and again, as in a bad dream, in a contest on Scheria that defines him as an athlete, but also as a spiritual seeker throughout his journey. His description as a man of "many turns" separates him from all other warriors of his time by acknowledging his complex nature, the excellence of his mind, his body, and his spirit. Attention to both his inner life and his outer life is what allows him to return home a wiser husband, father, and king.

In this way, Odysseus became the supreme example in classical literature of what George Leonard calls "the ultimate warrior," the one who conquers himself or herself. The qualities Odysseus portrays are, of course, mythic, larger than life, which is the enduring strength of Homer's epic tale. He is an ideal model. Yet it is tantalizing to consider ourselves on our own odyssey, lost and unable to find our way home unless we accept the final challenge, until we test ourselves in the heat of some kind of competition.

The point of overlap between myth, drama, and athletics is the inevitable ordeal at the heart of every adventure, the tests and trials we must pass if we are to make it back to our true home. This overarching philosophy suffused the sanctuaries across Greece, where temple, theater, and stadium were set side by side, underscoring the interrelatedness of religion, art, and athletics. The Greeks saw that all three aspects of life needed to be dramatized on a regular and ritual basis if this approach was going to be, as we say today, driven home.

For those of us seeking clues to the origins of the Olympic spirit, the classical concept of *arete* goes a long way in explaining the burning drive to achieve or witness excellence. And for those of us concerned about the Olympic spirit's perilous condition in the face of specters like genetic engineering for athletes of the future and exclusive "Jock Schools" to train youngsters for the Olympics, the notion of pursuing excellence for its own sake can be like a long drink of fresh water after a hard workout. A welcome counterpoise.

The need to argue for the value of excellence is not a modern-day phenomenon. Its value was articulated by Aristotle in *Politics*, in a passage that could have been written yesterday for a local school board meeting: "Not everyone agrees about what the young ought to learn and whether the goals should be *arete* or the good life, nor is it clear whether studies should be directed toward the development of intellect or character . . . It is necessary to define as vulgar any pursuit or craft or science which renders useless the body or soul or mind of free men for the practice of *arete* . . . It is therefore clear that there is an aspect of education that ought to be taught to our sons not because it is useful or necessary, but because it frees the spirit and ennobles the soul."

Reinvigorating our definition of winning with the ancient Greek understanding of *arete* can help us, not because it leads to glory, fame, or shoe contracts, but because "it frees the spirit and ennobles the soul." Carried this way, the Olympic fire lights up the darkness rather than burns those it touches.

THE EXCELLENT EFFORT

On its long ride through history to reach us, the word *arete* was translated by Latin scholars as *excellere*, which came to mean the effort to surpass oneself. *Excellere* is also the source of *exhilaration*, a word that is related to *hilaris*, cheerful. Together, these associations provide us with a clear, useful, and healthy ideal of excellence for sports. The excellent performance is the exhilarating effort that brings good cheer or supreme satisfaction because the athlete or artist has surpassed himself or herself in a moment of truth by dint of effort, courage, and enthusiasm.

Theosophist Shirley Nicholson discovered a raffish reference to the notion of athletes reaching their "higher potential" in Garry Trudeau's legendary comic strip. "An episode of 'Doonesbury,'" she writes, "shows a teenage girl at the beach with her boyfriend who is wearing his football helmet while lying on the sand. She tells him that her past-life experiences might make more sense to him if he himself would access his 'karmic core.' All he has to do is to ask himself who he really is in his present incarnation. He says, 'Easy. I'm a third-string quarterback.' She says that is fine, but what about his higher, spiritual self. 'A first-string quarterback.' Delighted, she tells him, 'See, you recognize the god within.'"

"The god within," of course, is the root meaning of *enthusiasm,* and is also, Nicholson notes, "the source of our untapped spiritual potentials and special abilities."

Artists and athletes, coaches and business managers alike are intimately familiar with the connection between enthusiasm and excellence. Emerson said, "Nothing great is achieved without enthusiasm," which is echoed by soccer immortal Pele: "Enthusiasm is everything. It must be as taut and vibrating as a guitar string."

Classical philosopher, scientist, and sports enthusiast Aristotle placed the excellent condition of body and soul at the center of his philosophy. In *De Anima* (On the human soul), he wrote a brilliant synopsis of the lapidary nature of *arete,* which he broke down to four excellences in the soul and four equivalent excellences in the body. He writes, in Thomas Cleary's translation, "Wisdom in the soul has its physical equivalent in perfection. Justice in the soul has its physical equivalent in beauty. Courage in the soul has its physical equivalent in strength. Modesty in the soul has its physical equivalent in health." Aristotle's observation about the interconnectedness of all aspects of human nature contrasts dramatically with our own unfortunate, artificial division between mind, body, and spirit.

The Greek emphasis on excellence may have been a strong motivation for Olympic athletes, but it proved a source of consternation for many critics. In the second century B.C.E., Lucian described what must have been a contemporary concern about the worthiness of the athletic festivals in the form of a dialogue between the ruler Solon and the poet Anacharsis. Solon tells the skeptical scrivener that he would not be wasting his time if he attended one of the events at Olympia, Nemea, or Athens: "You would learn for yourself, sitting in the middle of the crowd, watching the *arete* of men and physical beauty, amazing conditioning and great skill and irresistible force and daring and pride and unbeatable determination and indescribable passion for victory. I know that you would not stop praising and cheering and applauding."

The poet, like many intellectuals and clerics in our time, remains unconvinced, but his skepticism is healthy, as are the current complaints among modern critics. "I see," he scoffs, "that all these things—*arete* and conditioning and beauty and daring—are a waste since there is no purpose to them." He then asks whether all the competitors receive prizes, as if that would rationalize all the hard training.

"Not at all," replies Solon, laconically. "Only one among them—the victor."

The cynical poet is of course flabbergasted at the glaring absence of ample reward. To him, a crown of olive, laurel, celery, or pine, or possibly a jar of olive oil, is hardly enough to make the effort worthwhile. Yet the elemental satisfaction of a simple prize was exactly the point. Similarly, Herodotus tells us of a Persian general, at the battle of Thermopylae, who was in awe of the Greek warriors, who had trained as athletes. He asked the Greek Mardonius, "What sort of men have you led us to fight against, who contend not for money but purely for the sake of excelling?"

The sort who believed that excellent effort was its own reward.

This transcendent notion of success—as opposed to the transmogrified one that dominates modern culture—has been admirably described by novelist, art collector, and sports enthusiast James Michener: "One of the most compelling groups of statues left us from the days of antiquity are those which show exhausted athletes, such as the Charioteer of Polyzalos. When you look today at such a statue, you cannot tell whether the man has won or lost; all you know is that he has just completed a grueling test of some kind and that he is content. These statues represent the finest aspect of sports, the personal depletion at the end of the game, the exhaustion that leads to re-creation. It is this that the competitor seeks."

Writing in *Earth, Air, Fire, and Water* about the parallels between Greek art and athletics, art critic and mythologist Alexander Eliot says:

> Their statues of athletes were meant to honor not men alone, but gods. In fact art and athletics were but two sides of a single radiance, the sunshine of the Greek soul: arete. The word translates as excellence but it implied a great deal more than being first and best. Arete, in any endeavor, carried with it the unmistakable bloom of perfection. It meant "firmly seizing the beautiful," as Aristotle said. It fulfilled what is swift, powerful, passionate, shining with the light of eternal grace. Godlike-ness was the athlete's real aim, and victory was his proof . . . The key to the ancient Greeks is arete: they strove to act like gods. And the key to Greek sculpture also is arete: earthborn grace and force so shaped to enhance a sacred place.

Creation and re-creation are linked by the desire to express oneself and the excellent effort. The *excellent effort*, the struggle to beat the odds, the determination to overcome, is what is most admired. The genius of the Games is their dramatization of the breakthrough belief that it is possible and desirable to surpass one's self through a passion for competition. And as David C. Young writes, "The physical contests remained the exemplar, human competition *par excellence*. They represent elementally and in microcosm the general Greek struggle to rise above man's essentially ephemeral, abject condition and what a man cannot ordinarily do. To compete in the nude underscored this symbolic test of the individual man. The man and all he could do were laid bare before all. Only performance and achievement counted."

Excellence through struggle is the essence of Greek genius. However, the ancient Greeks also understood the ephemeral nature of success, which is why Nike, their goddess of victory, is depicted with windswept garments, winged and forever fleeting. Her Roman counterpart was Victoria, who was worshipped in her own temple by both soldiers and athletes. With palm branch or garland in hand, she is forever on the move, the consummate reminder of the transience of triumph. William Blake expressed the mythic moment this way:

> He who binds himself to a joy
> Does the winged life destroy.
> But he who kisses the joy as it flies
> Lives in eternity's sun rise.

What do these immortal images mean to us here and now? What can they tell us about our obsession with gold, winning, and success?

REWEIGHING GOLD

Where's the gold? Or as the agent cries out in the movie *Jerry McGuire*, "Where's the money? Show me the money!"

Show me the money! Is this any way to measure our greatest efforts, our striving for excellence? Is there no purpose, no satisfaction, in silver or bronze, in second or third—or last—place? "No gold, no glory—no endorsement contract," as one recent Olympic silver medalist bitterly complained.

To believe in the exact equation of gold and success is to commit what depth psychologist James Hillman calls "the sin of literalism." How can our athletes and coaches escape the trap of concretizing gold's mythic image, which leads inexorably to winning at any cost, and to debilitating shame for anyone who is not crowned a champion? Is there another image of gold that could lead us back to the Games' true spirit?

One ingenious alternative has been suggested by modern-day peripatetic philosopher Ronald Gross. In his seminars around the world, he regales audiences with accounts of the ambiguous feelings Socrates sparked in the citizens of Athens. Socrates' friends were always at a loss when it came to introducing the homely and unkempt philosopher to others: "They explained that Socrates was like the little statues of the [wise satyr] Silenus, which Athenian craftsmen sold in the agora. These plaster figures portrayed an ugly, drunken, dissolute, paunchy figure. But *inside* some of these little figurines, the sculptors imbedded a lovely golden figurine. The problem was that to discover the possible prize within your Silenus you had to be willing to break it open, smashing through the external mold to get at the inner treasure. Getting to know Socrates was like that, his friends said. You needed to be willing to get past the external appearance, to appreciate the soul within."

Socrates relished his role as social gadfly. To politicians, generals, athletes, and storekeepers alike he broke the bad news that they weren't as wise or successful as they thought. Our lives have a deeper purpose, he insisted, and to discover it we must dig below superficial appearances and discover what really matters, the inner gold. To do this he advocated strengthening both body and soul.

A carrier of the Socratic torch in our time is John Wooden, the most successful basketball coach in history. He would rarely speak about winning to his players or the media; instead he emphasized sports as a way of strengthening character and preparing yourself for the greater game of life. Similarly, Vince Lombardi emphasized: "The spirit, the will to win, and the will to excel are the things that endure. These qualities are much more important than the events that occur." As playfully as ever, comedienne Mae West agreed: "The score never interested me, only the game."

For those who contend that de-emphasizing winning may lead to a losing attitude, the annals of Olympic lore are full of passages from champions who argue the contrary. Four-time gold medalist John Naber writes, "The motto of the Olympic movement doesn't idolize the excellent, it encourages the devoted... Their wonderful and enlightening stories bring to life the timeless truths inherent in the pursuit of excellence through hard work, discipline and strong character. The message hidden just beneath the surface... is that Olympic champions are not extraordinary people, rather, they are ordinary people who merely have been able to accomplish extraordinary things."

The people's favorite from the Atlanta Games, gold-medal-winning gymnast Kerri Strug, has openly discussed the need to see through the superficial glamour of the Olympics to discover their deeper meaning. "Everyone is focusing on 'You're an Olympic champion,' but it's a lot more than that," she said. "We are representing our sport. We have a larger role to play... Gymnastics taught me how to be focused and disciplined, which helped me prepare for life."

What does a mythic reading of excellence mean in the current world of high-stakes competition, where winning a gold medal can lead to millions of dollars in endorsements? Who are the torch-bearers of excellence in the recent Olympiads, and what life lessons can we learn from them?

To find them, Naber writes in *Awakening the Olympian Within,* we need only search for the "stories of determination—where Olympians had a reason for giving up, but never did." As an Olympics broadcaster he discovered that viewers remembered those performances more than others. "What do these Olympians share in common besides their medals? They share an undying faith in the eventual positive outcome and an unwillingness to give up."

THE FLOW OF EXCELLENCE

Early in 1980, the Olympic spirit was lying about as low as the ancient athlete statues at the bottom of Homer's "wine dark sea." The Soviet Union had invaded Afghanistan, which instigated both a bellicose attitude and a boycott movement against the upcoming Summer Games in Moscow. But for a few days in late February, at the Lake Placid Winter Games, the Olympic spirit was bolstered when a group of unknown American college ice hockey players took on a grizzled team of Soviet professionals in the semifinals.

The young Americans had been whipped into shape by months of torturous workouts, which were low-lighted by hours of windsprints up and down the ice that the players derisively called "Herbies," after their coach, Herb Brooks. Described as a combination of Vince Lombardi, Bobby Knight, and Knute Rockne, Brooks was a ruthless disciplinarian—with a hidden heart of gold. His method and his vision appeared to be sheer madness: to beat the world champion Soviets at their own game—their superhuman conditioning.

En route to their classic matchup, the young Americans had tied Sweden, then beaten Czechoslovakia, Norway, Romania, and West Germany. In the locker room before the confrontation with the Soviets, Brooks became so emotional he had to *read* the ritual inspirational speech to his team: "You were born to be a player. You were meant to be here at this time. This is your moment." The team was shocked but slowly realized why he had pushed them so hard. They hadn't been expected to even reach the qualifying round, and now they were poised to win the whole shebang, if only they could beat the world champion Soviets. They stood a chance only if they were in better condition than any other team, had tougher discipline, and if they played with more heart.

The Yanks fell behind early but tied the score, 2–2, with one second to go at the end of the first period. The crowd was electrified as an upset loomed as a distinct possibility. They filled the arena with ecstatic cries of "USA! USA!" Two minutes into the second period the Americans fell behind again, 3–2, but Jim Craig, their stouthearted goalie, held on for the rest of the period. Astonishingly, at the 8:39 mark of the third period, Mark Johnson scored to tie the game, and the impossible suddenly seemed possible. With only ten minutes left, their captain, Mike Eruzione, stole the puck and fired a wrist shot on goal from twenty-five feet out.

"The puck could be seen hopping like a tadpole," writes Al Silverman, as it skipped past the stunned Soviet goalie. All the young Americans had to do now was keep the greatest hockey players in the world from scoring for ten long minutes—an eternity in hockey time.

"Play your game! Play your game! Play your game!" bellowed Brooks. Eruzione took that to mean: "It was all about maintaining speed and skills and puck movement and using the freedom he'd given us to be creative." Which they did. They tenaciously held back the great red tide of jerseys as the Soviets tried desperately to tie the score. With five seconds left, the play-by-play announcer, Al Michaels, shouted in exultation, "Do you believe in miracles?" Then the buzzer sounded and he answered his own question by shouting a triumphant "Yesssss! The impossible dream comes true!"

A few days later, E. M. Swift wrote a perceptive piece, "The Lesson and Message of What We Can Be," for *Sports Illustrated*, which is nearly as famous in the annals of sportswriting as the victory is in Olympic lore. It reads in part:

> For millions of people, their single, lasting image of the Lake Placid Games will be the infectious joy displayed by the U.S. hockey team following its 4–3 win over the Soviet Union . . . It was an Olympian moment . . . the kind the creators of the Games must have had in mind, one that said: Here is something that is bigger than any of you. It was bizarre, it was beautiful. Upflung sticks slowly cart-wheeled into the rafters . . . The Soviet players, slightly in awe, it seemed, of the spectacle of their defeat, stood in a huddle near their blue line, arms propped on their sticks . . . There was no head-hanging. This was bigger, even, than the Russians. "The first Russian I shook hands with had a smile on his face," said Mark Johnson, who had scored two of the U.S. goals. "I couldn't believe it. I still can't believe it. We beat the Russians."

And for many that day, the "infinite moment" was the sight of the U.S. goalie Jim Craig skating around after the victory, flag draped over his shoulder, mouthing the words, "Where is my father?" The utter joy on his face when he finally saw his dad in the stands is an iconic moment in Olympic history. It reminds us that the ancient athletes often competed more for their family and city-state than for themselves, and that the thrill of victory is incomplete unless it's shared with those we love. How else could the fairy tale on ice have ended?

The Russian player's smile at Mark Johnson surely reflects

the Olympic spirit of goodwill that occasionally transcends national boundaries. But the image of the players leaning on their sticks, immobile but dignified in defeat, reflects the universal response of wonder for the kind of selfless team play and boundless enthusiasm shown by their opponents. In the flow of moments like these is the capacity for joy—even in loss—*if* players, coaches, and spectators alike recognize that the sport is bigger than any one team, any one player, that what makes a great game possible is the excellence of the competition.

The beauty and power of this shift of philosophy is that it takes pressure off the single athlete—a pressure that produces narcissism and even the recent phenomenon of "fan rage"—and places the focus back where it belongs, on the game itself.

Lest we forget that this magnanimous spirit can also be expressed in the moment of one's greatest glory, let's recall that day, in 1936, when Jesse Owens was crowned with his first laurel wreath. He delivered a lesson for the ages. Rather than dwell on his own achievement, he looked straight into the movie cameras, smiled, and redirected the attention back to the other athletes by saying simply, "Thanks for the grand competition."

THE SELFLESS SECRET OF SUCCESS

For the Twenty-Third Olympiad, in 1984, Los Angeles attempted to fulfill one of Coubertin's unfulfilled Olympic dreams. "The Games must be more intimate," he once said, "and, above all . . . less expensive." Like the U.S. hockey team in 1980, the Los Angeles organizers achieved what most observers had believed impossible or improbable, at best. Under the tutelage of Peter Ueberroth, Los Angeles's baseball commissioner from 1984 to 1989, they convinced thirty corporations to pay the $4 million fee to become official sponsors, which helped build new sporting complexes and refurbish the Memorial Coliseum, and garnered a record $225 million from ABC television for exclusive television rights. While risking charges of overcommercializing the Games, the organizers avoided the monstrous debts incurred by both Montreal and Moscow. They also became the first host city to post a profit, calculated at a formidable $200 million.

One ingenious innovation that helped counteract the charges of commodification was the ten-week Olympics Art Festival. The lavishly orchestrated fete featured one hundred exhibitions and performances from nearly two dozen countries, including the Korean National Dance Company and the Royal Opera of Covent Garden, the Circus Oz of Australia, and China's Central Ensemble of National Music. The unforgettable opening ceremonies in the Coliseum featured a jet-propelled "rocket man" and were capped off by a 960-voice choir accompanied by eighty-four baby grand pianos. Even so, Hollywood style did not necessarily triumph over Olympic substance.

The L.A. Games were highlighted by Great Britain's extraordinary gliding middle-distance runner, Sebastian Coe, who captured his second straight 1,500-meter title, and the incomparably graceful Greg Louganis, who won diving titles in the platform and springboard events. The women's high jump title was won by Germany's Ulrike Meyfarth—who had become the youngest women's high jump champion at the Munich Games, in 1972. Twelve years later, at age twenty-eight, she outwomaned Italy's Sara Simeoni by clearing 6 feet, 7½ inches, making her also the oldest woman high jump champion in Olympic history. In the 400-meter hurdles, Edwin Moses extended his winning streak to an astonishing 102 straight races. Canada won its first gold medal in swimming when Alex Baumann, with a red maple leaf tattooed on his chest, won the 400-meter individual medley.

© IOC/Olympic Museum Collections

Greg Louganis in 1984. At the 1996 Atlanta Games, he won two gold medals and an Olympic Spirit Award for his courageous performance after a serious head injury on the diving board.

The first Olympic women's marathon was won by two-time Boston Marathon champion Joan Benoit, despite the fact that she was still recovering from arthroscopic knee surgery as well as an operation on her Achilles tendon and a painful hamstring pull. Benoit ran a courageous race, outlasting an opponent who had beaten her in ten out of eleven races, Norway's Grete Waitz. Her winning time was the third fastest ever by a woman—2:24:52.

"When I came into the stadium," she recalled, "and saw all the colors and everything, I told myself, 'Listen, just look straight ahead because if you don't you're going to faint.'"

Sprinter Valerie Briscoe-Hooks became a folk hero of another order—a world-class athlete-parent. After she won three gold medals, in the 200- and 400-meter races and in the 4 x 400-meter relay, she told prospective Olympians that it is possible to excel in two things at once: "You can do both: be a great parent and a great professional. It takes more effort, but trust me, it's worth it." In true Olympic spirit, she has parleyed her fame and wisdom into a sports mentoring program in Los Angeles called "Peer to Peer."

Two other individuals articulated the deeper implications of athletic success at these Games: track and field superstar Carl Lewis and gymnast Bart Connor. Lewis matched his hero Jesse Owens's four gold medals by winning the 100- and 200-meter races, the 4 x 100-meter relay, and the long jump. Afterwards Lewis said, "Well, I feel there are no limitations if you broaden your horizons. If you don't succeed you haven't failed, because you can't fail if you've tried your hardest. So I hope I can just be remembered as someone who inspired people and led them to do things they never thought they could do."

Connor completed his long odyssey to Olympic victory by snaring two gold medals at UCLA's Pauley Pavilion. His feat was particularly meaningful to those who recalled that the boycott of the Moscow Games had nearly crushed his spirits. Instead of wallowing in self-pity, he trained harder than ever for the 1984 Games, despite debilitating injuries and ferocious competition— and barely made the American Olympic team.

When sportswriter Charlie Jones asked him how he had found the fortitude to claw his way back, Connor credited his parents, but not just for their generic family support.

"As long as I can remember," he told Jones, "every night when I went to bed, either my mother or my father sat with me and asked,

'What did you do today that was a success?' As a kid, maybe it was a crayon drawing, or perhaps as I got a little older it was A-B-C, not the whole alphabet, but just the first three letters, A-B-C, or maybe it was when I was a little bit older and did my first back flip off the living room couch, but every night we would always review the day and pick out one thing in which I was successful. So every night of my life I have gone to bed a successful man."

Conner used this method of positive reinforcement and visualization while rehabilitating himself after his injuries. Rather than focusing on his pain and misfortune, he would isolate the one detail that revealed even minute improvement, even incremental progress. Then he would remind himself of his steady improvement when he went to bed, ensuring that he went to sleep "a successful man."

Charlie Jones remarks, "What a great lesson that is, because all of us, every day, have our successes. We just need to remind ourselves of that fact and then take them to sleep with us every night as a successful person."

Together, Jones and Connor remind us that the road to excellence is gradual, steady, faithful, courageous. While we may not all possess the fast-twitch muscle fibers of the sprinter, the lung capacity of the long-distance swimmer, or the flexible tendons of the gymnast, what the great Olympic tales tell us is that we all possess *genius*, a *daimon*, a higher force or spirit that speaks to us, pulls us forward, encourages us to make an *excellent effort*. What motivated the ancients still moves us today, the belief that our honest effort—no matter how difficult—is transformed into joy by the desire to excel. Beyond the obvious and literal aim of winning is the goal of excellence itself. After all, says John Wooden, "who can ask more of a man than giving all within his span? Giving all, it seems to me, is not so far from victory."

Coach Wooden has spent years refining his definition of success to near-mythic status in the worlds of both sports and business: "Success is peace of mind attained only through self-satisfaction in knowing you've made the effort to do the best of which you're capable."

Four years after his fourth-place finish in the men's 500-meter speed-skating competition at the 1984 Sarajevo Winter Games, Dan Jansen, world speed-skating champion, was expected to bring home the gold in both the 500- and 1,000-meter races at the Winter Games in Calgary. But personal tragedy struck the day of the 500 meters. His sister, Jane Beres, died from leukemia. Understandably distracted, Jansen slipped on the ice in both time trials and could not even finish. Undeterred, he trained for the next Olympiad, the 1992 Winter Games in Albertville, France. Jansen was again predicted to win, but again a mishap doomed him. He finished fourth, thirty-two-hundredths of a second from third place and the bronze.

At the press conference before Jansen's fourth appearance in Olympic competition, at the 1994 Olympic Winter Games in Lillehammer, Norway, a caustic reporter declared, "You realize that if you come out of these Olympics without a medal again, you'll probably go down in history as the greatest speed skater *never* to have won an Olympic medal." Cool as the ice he loved to skate on, Jansen replied, "That's one way to look at it, but I choose to look at it another way. With this being my fourth Olympic Games, I have also had the opportunity to become one of the most *successful* Olympians of all time."

As if living out the advice from the Arabian Nights tales, that "where you fall, there is your gold," in his eighth and last Olympic race Dan Jansen stumbled again—but this time he recovered. Skating his heart out in the 1,000 meters, he took first place and set a world record in 1:12:43.

"For me, success is very private and very personal," he told John Naber years later. "It means being able to look back after a big race, presentation, quarter, etc., and know that you did everything you could to prepare yourself and that you gave it your best effort. Winning is terrific and it's what any competitive person strives for, but it should not be the *only* measure of success." His own gold standard sums up his remarkably stoic philosophy: "I do not try to be better than anyone else. I only try to be better than myself."

During his victory lap, before an exultant crowd of 10,000, Jansen cradled his baby daughter in his arms. Her name is Jane, after his sister.

THE SEOUL OF THE GAMES

At the 1988 Games in Seoul, South Korea, twenty-seven new world records were set and spectacular new stars appeared in the Olympic firmament. East German Kristin Otto swam her way to six gold medals—one less than Mark Spitz's record haul in 1972 and one more than "the Big Fish," American swimmer Matt Biondi, who captured five golds, a silver, and a bronze at Seoul. Biondi's sly explanation for his second-place finish to Anthony Nesty of Surinam in the 100-meter butterfly underscores the often infinitesimal measurements that make the difference in Olympic competition. "I guess I shouldn't have cut my fingernails. That might make up for one-hundredths of a second."

The most glamorous athlete of the Seoul Games was an American bank teller, beautician, and sprinter who captured the attention of the world by running with long, painted fingernails and in what she called her "athletic negligees"—dazzling, often diaphanous, racing uniforms. The seeming limitlessness of her talents was part of her personal mythology. As a school girl, Florence Griffith-Joyner, or "Flo-Jo," was asked what she wanted to be when she grew up. "I want to be an actor, a designer, and I want to go to the Olympics." Her teacher told her she could only choose one thing, which angered her, for her mother had said she could be *anything* she wanted to be. Flo-Jo said that as soon as her mother heard what happened, "she confronted the teacher and told her she couldn't put limits on my life." In Seoul, still defiant and determined to overcome any limits thrown her way, including exercise-induced asthma, she won gold medals in the 100 and 200 meters and as a member 4 x 100-meter relay team, plus a silver as part of the 4 x 400-meter relay team.

In his memoirs, 1956 Olympic basketball champion and fourteen-time All-Star Bill Russell says, perhaps presciently, "If you could bottle all the emotion let loose in a basketball game, you'd have enough hate to fight a war and enough joy to prevent one."

The American basketball team entered the Seoul Games with an 85–1 record in Olympic play, having lost the still-contested finals match to the Soviet Union in 1972. In the semifinals at Seoul, the Americans lost a fiercely played game to the Soviets, 82–76. The loss was the final straw that prompted the U.S. sports establishment to eventually allow the best American players—the professionals in the NBA—to play for their country, just as the best players in other countries were able to perform for theirs.

In December, 2002, I interviewed Sarunas Marciulionis, one of the three Lithuanians who had played on the 1988 Soviet team and later the first foreign player to be drafted by the NBA. Over pints of Guinness at O'Reilly's pub in San Francisco, I asked Marciulionis what had really motivated the team. Did the game have political or cultural overtones? Was there an undercurrent of bitterness towards the Americans because they refused to admit they had lost to the Soviets in 1972? Were they insulted that the silver medal lies unclaimed to this day in the Olympic offices in Lausanne?

Sarunas patiently shook his head no to all my questions, then became impassioned as he recounted one of the turning points in his life—and in the history of Olympic competition.

"This was the Olympics," he said. "Our first goal was to win against the Americans—but not for Soviet pride. We had another purpose. For us, winning was a personal ticket to freedom, but we thought maybe also freedom for the world. We wanted to win because there was no other proof of what country is stronger without nuclear war. In sports you see the results right away, who is stronger. In politics you must wait and wait and wait. Back then—before *perestroika*—we knew we couldn't wait much longer."

Marciulionis paused, then said, "We knew we had an opportunity to show the world that two countries could compete with each other without going to war, that you can fight for your country and still show respect for the other country you are competing against."

The 1992 Barcelona Olympics were the first in three decades that were not beset by boycott. More than 10,000 athletes from 197 nations competed, including Cuba, North Korea, and South Africa, who were once more invited into the Olympic fold. For the first time, the Baltic states of Lithuania, Latvia, and Estonia sent teams under their own flags. Bhutan was represented by a team of archers who had never before seen an airplane or the ocean. Greece won its first medal since the 1896 Games, through the talents of Paraskevi Patoulido in the women's 100-meter hurdles. Carl Lewis won two more gold medals—one in the 400-meter relay and his third consecutive in the long jump. The host country, Spain, celebrated its own Fermin Cacho Ruiz's victory in the 1,500 meters.

Considered the strongest man in the world—pound for pound—weightlifter Naim Suleymanoglu, all of four feet, eleven inches tall and 140 pounds, a native of Bulgaria who defected to Turkey, had first competed for his new homeland at the 1988 Seoul Games. Nicknamed "Turkish delight," he entered the featherweight event and broke the world record in both the snatch and the jerk, winning his first gold medal. At the Barcelona Games the firebrand lifter outdueled his former countryman, Nikolay Peshalov, and became renowned for his fearlessness.

At the 1981 Olympic Congress, the nettlesome phrase "Olympic amateur" had been stricken from the Olympic charter. In the early 1990s, the IOC finally allowed professionals to compete for their country if their governing sports federations agreed. This was the dramatic setup for creation of "the Dream Team," one of the most talented and colorful basketball teams of all time, featuring eleven stellar players from the NBA, including Michael Jordan, Magic Johnson, and Larry Bird, and one college player, Christian Laettner.

Victorino Cunham, an awestruck player on the Angolan Olympic basketball team, when asked if he remembered the moment he knew what his own team was up against, replied, "In the airport when I saw the first five USA players get off the plane." The Dream Team's coach, Chuck Daly, said, "It was like traveling with twelve rock stars."

Led by Jordan, whose legendary work ethic, competitive fire, pride, and passion for the game helped revolutionize basketball and bring it to the attention of the entire world, the team steamrollered over the opposition, laying its final stake for the gold medal with a win over Spain, 96–55. Afterwards, the effervescent Magic Johnson captured the elusive magic of the Games: "It's sort of hard to put into words what [winning the Olympics] means . . . I've won every championship there is to win. You can throw them all in a hat, and it'll never compare to this."

As impressive as the victory was, there was ample grumbling over the team's seeming effortless win and their decision to reside in separate hotels away from the rest of the Olympic athletes.

In contrast to the silky-smooth but drama-less triumph of the Dream Team was the impassioned performance by the underdog team from newly liberated Lithuania. In the years between the Seoul and Barcelona Games, Lithuania had broken away from the Soviet Union, and Marciulionis had seized the day by quickly assembling a team to play in 1992.

"Those of us on the 1988 team who weren't *Russian* felt satisfaction," Marciulionis told me, "but no *joy* because we were not fighting for *our* country—Lithuania." Basketball, he reminded me, is like a second religion in his homeland, and now they had a chance to play David against the Soviet Goliath. Money was scarce for food, water, rent, or even vodka, not to speak of basketball. However, Marciulionis had just been drafted by the Golden State Warriors, so he appealed to his newfound friends in the San Francisco Bay Area—the Grateful Dead. The Dead sent the funds necessary to field the team, partially raised by sales of a tie-dye T-shirt featuring a basketball-dribbling skeleton. The shirt became one of the most sought-after souvenirs of the Barcelona Games after "Lithu-mania" spread through the Olympic Village.

The Lithuanian basketball team, sporting their Grateful Dead T-shirts, celebrate their second bronze medal at the 1996 Atlanta Games.

"After all those years of those Soviet colors (in daily life), nothing but blues and grays," said Marciulionis, "the guys went nuts for those shirts. They ended up wearing them to bed, to practice, everywhere."

Led by Marciulionis and seven-foot-four-inch center Arvydis Sabonis, who was playing for the Portland Trailblazers, the Lithuanians stunned the sporting world by wrenching away the bronze medal from their heavily favored rivals, the Russians. The incredible upset was comparable to a team from a small-sized state like Maine thumping a team assembled from all the rest of the American states combined.

As C. W. Nevius wrote in his column for the *San Francisco Chronicle*, "When they won that game, there was delirium in Lithuania, not to mention the team's locker room. 'The guys went crazy,' said assistant coach Donny Nelson, 'and then all of a sudden everybody quieted down. And at that moment the President of the country walked in and everybody started singing the national anthem. There wasn't a dry eye in the place.'"

The players' profound response to winning the bronze medal had to do, Marciulionis says, with the satisfaction that comes from "the small, steady steps that lead to *excellence*." And the joy from the excellence, he adds, derives from "loving the steps of the game."

However, if you forget to enjoy the day-by-day details of the game, play only for yourself, or for the wrong team, or only for money, it can destroy your love for the game and more.

"If you play for the wrong reasons, then you cannot love your life," he told me with the same enthusiasm he had once displayed on the basketball court. "You must play for something bigger than yourself, and only then can you feel the *real spirit* of the Olympics. Each person in the Olympics has a different motivation—opportunity, money, recognition—but we played for *love of the game*. We trained for so many years for something over those other motives because you get swallowed up by them. You have to play for the greater good, the *challenge* to be recognized, as an athlete or a country."

Winning the first Olympic medal was a kind of "soul food" for the Lithuanians, says Marciulionis. "It fed our people at a time when we were physically hungry because we had just broken away from the Soviet Union, but we were also spiritually hungry. It sounds strange, but winning gave us an identity when no one in the world knew who or where we were."

The basketball team's scintillating performance at the Barcelona Games released the long pent-up spirit of the land. Four years later, at the 1996 Atlanta Games, and again in the 2000 Sydney Games, this small but passionate and poetic country carried on its independence celebrations by winning two more bronze medals.

The honor of staging the Centennial Games, slated for 1996, was a bitter cultural and economic battle between Athens and Atlanta. In the end, "Coca-Cola won over the Parthenon," as the Greek Minister of Culture Melina Mercouri commented sardonically. Despite the international grumbling, Atlanta launched what Mayor Billy Payne promised would be the most peaceful Games in history and the most exemplary of the true Olympic vision: "To compete is the highest form of victory."

The Atlanta Games were replete with memorable Olympic moments. Irish eyes were smiling when Ireland's swimmer Michelle Smith won three gold medals and a bronze—more than her country's teams had won in all of Olympic history. The weightlifting competition saw a "three"-peat in the featherweight event by the "Pocket Hercules," Turkey's Naim Suleymanoglu, who outdueled Valerios Leonidis of Greece with a winning lift of 413 pounds, an almost incomprehensible three times his own body weight.

In the long jump competition, Carl Lewis performed what journalist Pico Iyer has called "an act of self-transcendence that took my breath away." On his third jump, he soared 27 feet, 7½ inches, which launched him into the lead by a startling eight inches. "Then with the air of godly entitlement," writes Iyer, "that not always endeared him to his rivals, he simply sat back and watched them try, one after another, to beat him (and fail). Imperial to the end, he even declined to take his final jump, as if it were not worth his time to try to improve on his lead." Iyer reports that at the press conference that followed Lewis's victory—his fourth straight Olympic win in the long jump and ninth overall gold medal—Lewis looked as dazzled as everyone else. Smiling at the clutch of cameras in the room, he finally said, "What are you guys all doing in my dream?"

The 10,000-meter race pitted Ethiopian long distance runner Haile Gebrselassie against Kenya's Paul Tergat. Gebrselassie had began his career running barefoot twelve miles a day from the family farm to school and back. His later running style—with his left arm crooked—is a holdover from his boyhood runs with his schoolbooks cradled in his arm. When he toed the starting line in Atlanta he was the reigning world-record holder in his specialty, the 10,000 meters, and two-time world champion. As expected, it was a fierce contest for the first 8,000 meters. Then Tergat pulled away from the pack, with Gebrselassie close behind until the last few meters, when Gebrselassie won by two long strides.

As film critic Roger Ebert wrote in his review of *Endurance*, the eminently inspiring movie based on Gebrselassie's life, "The secret of his greatness, we gather, is that he ran and ran, longer and harder than anyone else, until in his big race he was simply the best prepared. [He is] a runner whose triumph must be explained almost entirely from within his own determination." The film ends memorably with that Olympic run, Gebrselassie

Sidney, Australia, September 25, 2000: two-time gold-winner in the 1,500-meter run, and the pride of Ethiopia, Haile Gebrselassie.

triumphantly breaking the tape in 27:07:34, only one second ahead of Tergat, who is followed closely by Salah Hissou of Morocco. Then all three exhausted runners walk away over the infield grass, backs to the camera, arms around each other's shoulders, in a brilliant cameo of the dream of Olympic brotherhood.

Nineteenth-century American bard Walt Whitman, an inveterate baseball fan, wrote, "Yes, Victory is great sometimes [but] when it cannot be helped, Defeat is also great. No victory is great when it is bought at the sacrifice of ideals; and no defeat is disgraceful as long as one does his best and follows the gleam of idealism." After an over-the-top media buildup comparing him to Jim Thorpe, American decathlete Dan O'Brien was stricken with anxiety during the Olympic trials for the Barcelona Games. He suffered the worst conceivable indignity for an athlete of his caliber: he was left home after being unable to clear the bar on his final pole vault attempt.

In *Competitive Fire*, Michael Clarkson writes that O'Brien trained hard for the next four years so he could compete in the Atlanta Games. He and his trainers seem to have recognized the value of the ancient Olympic model of total excellence—mind and soul as well as body. O'Brien added a sports psychologist, Jim Reardon, to his coaching staff to help him with relaxation techniques. "The first thing O'Brien did was to realize that having fears and anxieties are normal among elite athletes facing pressure situations, that he didn't have to be a nonfeeling superman." During the interim years he won all eight decathlons in which he competed.

O'Brien commented, "I took some of the importance out of it by saying to myself this wasn't for the gold medal, but for my personal pride. I couldn't care what others thought any more. I only cared about what I thought of myself. We have to learn to deal with our egos." To accomplish this leap of faith, he practiced a sophisticated form of visualization infused with what anthropologists call *participation mystique*, an approach to ritual practice in which the line between the participant and the rite is nearly nonexistent. "I took one jump, one throw, one run at a time," O'Brien said later. "I tried to *become* each event."

Not only did O'Brien transcend the fear and reconcile the personal anxiety that had crippled him four years before, but he also won the gold medal and set an Olympic decathlon record of 8,824 points.

Despite Mayor Payne's promise, the Olympics' perennial dream of peaceful competition was shattered by the explosion of an anonymous terrorist bomb in Centennial Park. But after the initial panic and dread, the Games continued. The courageous performance by an Iranian-born, American-raised super-heavyweight Greco-Roman wrestler named Matt Ghadaffi personified the refusal of the entire Olympic movement to be intimidated. In the match of his life, Ghadaffi was pitted against the "Gentle Giant," Siberian folk hero Alexandr Karelin, also nicknamed "King Kong" and "the Experiment," generally regarded as the greatest wrestler in Olympic history. Defying the oddsmakers, Ghadaffi wrestled undefeated world champion Karelin to a draw in regulation time, only to lose 1–0, in overtime. Ghadaffi wept unabashedly on the silver-medal stand, saying later, "I wrestled my heart and soul out."

Fortunately, not all of his heart and soul.

Hours after the medal ceremony, Ghadaffi quietly slipped away from the festivities and visited the hospital where the victims of the bombing lay, becoming the first Olympian to spend time with them. At the hospital he shared his silver medal with Fallon Stubbs, who had lost his mother in the deadly explosion, a gesture which was later called an "enduring symbol of sportsmanship and compassion."

THE GAMES OF RECONCILIATION

The first Games of the new millennium were held in Sydney, Australia. A raucous crowd of 110,000 greeted the parade of twelve thousand athletes from two hundred nations and was then treated to a marvelously mythological opening ceremony that would have made the organizers of the ancient Games proud. Mort Rosenblum, senior Associated Press correspondent, described the ceremony as "a thunder of hoofbeats, wild fantasy, blazing color, and booming cheers from a moist-eyed crowd." For once, he wrote, there was a display of real Olympian brotherhood as Australia seized its moment in the global spotlight and "depicted its colorful history, from the indigenous 'dreaming' of creation to a hopeful future of varied cultures in a seamless society."

The dazzling ceremony, featuring fantasy fishes, magical dust, drums, didgeridoos, cleansing smoke, and fireworks, was followed by a historical moment with mythic implications. The Olympic torch was carried into the stadium by the brilliant Australian Aborigine sprinter Cathy Freeman.

"An estimated 3.7 billion people," wrote the *Christian Science Monitor*, "watched the Aboriginal runner jog up the steps to the giant cauldron in a white bodysuit Friday. And with a walk into a pool of water, where she lit a ring of bubbling gas jets, Australia sent a message to more than half the world." The message signaled the country's emergence as a vibrant, multicultural nation that is steadily reconciling with its native people, who have lived on that continent for at least forty thousand years. Thus this Olympiad's name, the Reconciliation Games.

"There has never been an occasion," said the *Sydney Herald*, "when more has been expected of an Australian sportsperson." Freeman was "beseeched by the nation" to mine for gold. Like all great athletes, she rose to the occasion, winning a thrilling 400-meter race in the record time of 49.11, and then fell to her knees, as if in a prayer of thanks. When she opened her eyes, 112,000 people were cheering her as if she were the answer to *their* prayers of reconciliation. When she ran her victory lap she carried both the Aboriginal and Australian flags.

The question remains, however, as Michael Gordon wrote afterward, "what impact Freeman's example of athletic excellence and unaffected generosity of spirit will have on young Australians, particularly those in indigenous communities which have had all too little to celebrate."

Beyond their symbolic import, these Games, like their predecessors, stirred the passions of fans around the world. The heroes ranged from the unlikeable to the unlikely. What they held in common, wrote *Time* magazine's Karl Taro Greenfeld, was that they were all in town "for exactly the same reason—to compete, baby, to compete."

And compete they did, led by Michael Johnson's custom-made 24-karat-gold running shoes, which carried him to a 43.87–second win in the 400 meters, making him the first to earn consecutive gold medals at that distance. Finland's Jan Zelezny became the only three-time Olympic champion in the javelin, out-throwing Great Britain's Steve Backley and setting an Olympic record for the third straight time. The Australian "Thorpedo," seventeen-year-old swimming sensation Ian Thorpe, described as being able to "move water like the moon," powered his way to three golds and a silver medal. In track and field, world-record holder in the 100 meters Maurice Greene, running into a strong headwind, still flashed to victory in the second fastest time in Olympic history, 9.87 seconds. Reigning world-record holder Haile Gebrselassie won his unprecedented second straight 10,000-meter race—and his second consecutive last-gasp victory over his Kenyan rival, Paul Tergat. This time around Tergat led until the last stride of the race when the stout-hearted Gebrselassie strode past him by a hair's breadth—0.9 seconds—making it the closest victory in the history of the event. Laura Wilkinson recovered from a severely fractured right foot to become the first American woman to win the platform diving competition since Lesley Bush, in 1964. Her upset over the heavily favored Chinese divers inspired her coach, Ken Armstrong, to say, "This is the Olympics. Magical things happen all the time."

America's world-record holder in the women's pole vault, Stacy Dragila, soared 15 feet, 1 inch to defeat Australia's own Tatyana Grigorieva. Afterwards, Steve Ruskin wrote a moving piece in *Sports Illustrated* that offers golden advice about the power of visualization to reduce anxiety. "The yearlong pressure of being the Olympic favorite," he writes, "had driven Dragila to spend long sessions lying in the dark, visualizing success in Sydney, and she did it again [before her event]. She saw the stadium, full and throbbing with energy, bathed in camera flashes. She saw herself sailing over the bar and hearing the roar. 'I saw beautiful things,' she said."

Inspired to become an athlete by watching Florence Griffith-Joyner in the 1984 Summer Olympics, Marion Jones had a stellar college career at the University of North Carolina in basketball and track and field. Showing why she was nicknamed "Hard Nails"—for her tenacious discipline and confidence—Jones came to Sydney and promptly announced her "Drive for Five." She planned to break Jesse Owens's and Carl Lewis's American records of four golds in one Olympiad, and match Paavo Nurmi's five-gold performance at the 1924 Paris Games. She won her 100- and 200-meter races and anchored the winning 200- and 400-meter relays, but placed second, behind 1992 Olympic champion Heike Drechsler of Germany, in the long jump. So she settled for a mere mortal haul of four golds rather than an immortal five. At the press conference, she expressed mild disappointment but quickly got over it, telling reporters, "The drive for five is not alive. I didn't regret it at all, I had a shot at it and it didn't pan out. Inside I'm disappointed but she deserved the gold."

After her first victory, in the 100 meters, Jones carried both the American and the Belize flags in honor of her mother, who hails from that Central American country. Shortly after the Games, she was awarded the Order of Belize, and in her acceptance speech Jones admitted she had been a bit brash to boast she would win five gold medals. Then she spoke candidly about her epiphany *while crossing the finish line*—one of the greatest of all Olympic lessons: that she was playing and competing for something larger than herself. "I still wondered, Why am I really doing this?" she told the audience. "I'm loving it. I'm having a ball, but there is something more. I can't really put my hand on it. And so [when] I crossed the finish line for the hundred meters—and I won, by the way—I immediately saw my family."

Her voice broke with emotion, and then she went on: "And then I knew what it was all about—it was all about family."

As Olympics filmmaker Bud Greenspan has determined, after thirty years of making documentaries about the Games, the champions aren't always the gold medal winners, and gold medal winners aren't always champions. This spirit was echoed over and over again during the Sydney Games. The Lithuanian basketball team lost to the Americans in the semifinals and then triumphed over Australia, 89–71, for the Lithuanians' third straight bronze medal. What would have been a disappointing result for some was a source of pride for Coach Jonas Kazlluskas and his players, who had an Olympic sense of proportion about their marvelous accomplishment. "It's no secret," he said, "we're happy with another bronze medal. We are pleased with what we did."

In a similar spirit of soulful pride, Australian basketball star Andrew Gaze had the immense honor of carrying his country's flag in the opening ceremony and then proceeding to play in his record-tying fifth Olympics. During the tournament he ran his career point total in the Games to 789, second only to that of Brazil's legendary Oscar Schmidt, 1,093. It wasn't enough to nudge his team onto the victory stand, and Australia finished out of the medals again, which meant his career concluded without an Olympic prize—but he steadfastly resisted any suggestion that it was all for naught.

"Obviously you want to win a medal," he remarked later. "The Olympics are all about opportunities I have had. You want the victories and you want the ultimate, but there's an awful lot you get along the way, whether it's the chance to share with players from other countries or to be part of the great teams that I have played with. The opportunity I have had to compete has been a reward in itself. I would certainly not say it was empty in any way. Conversely to that, it has been extremely full and I've been very, very happy to be a part of it."

Meanwhile, the U.S. men's basketball team lost a little of its swagger when it had to struggle throughout the tournament to dodge the humiliation of elimination. No longer were the other teams in awe, which moved American star guard Gary Payton to comment in surprise, "These guys don't even ask for autographs anymore." In the gold medal game, the United States hung on to beat Australia handily. However, warned one sardonic commentator, if the Yanks don't change tactics and take the competition more seriously, "the Parthenon is in danger of becoming 'the second most famous ruin at the Athens Games.'"

An intrinsic part of the charm of the Olympics is the emergence of the unlikely folk hero. In Sydney, this indispensable colorful character turned out to be a swimmer in the 100-meter freestyle heat who had only been swimming for nine months. Twenty-two-year-old Eric Moussambani, from Equatorial Guinea, had trained modestly: one hour a day, three days a week, in a 20-meter hotel pool near his Malabo home. As luck would have it, when the other two swimmers in his qualifying heat jumped the gun and were eliminated for their false start, Moussambani was forced to swim alone, except for the nearly four billion people watching him on television. His performance, and the response it evoked from the fans in the Aquatic Centre, recall the reflection by Malvolio, the steward in Shakespeare's *Twelfth Night*: "Some men are born great, some achieve greatness, and some have greatness thrust upon them."

In Moussambani's case, if it was not greatness of accomplishment, it was at least a certain greatness of effort, humor, and sense of proportion. His swimming technique and level of exhaustion as he hit the wall for the turnaround on his last lap worried at least one onlooker enough to strip down to his shorts, ready to dive into the pool to save the novice swimmer. That is when "Eric the Eel," as he was soon dubbed, resorted to his now infamous dog-paddle technique. He finished in 1:52, rather slower than the world record of 0:48, but when he touched the wall it was "to the loudest cheers the Games had yet heard."

Surrounded by the press and adoring fans at the end of the race, he said, "I want to send hugs and kisses to the crowd, because it was their cheering that kept me going."

Another crowd favorite was Rulon Gardner, a super-heavyweight wrestler in the Greco-Roman division, from the University of Nebraska. Gardner had defeated Matt Ghadaffi in the U.S. trials, which earned him the right to confront the still-undefeated Alexander Karelin, now aiming for his fourth straight Olympic gold medal.

The matchup at Sydney Exhibition Hall echoed the ancient Games, and not only because the event is called Greco-Roman. The excited press stories about the two wrestlers' training techniques evoked mythic memories of Milo of Croton, who trained as a young man by lifting young calves and gradually moved up to lifting mature cows when he was middle-aged and still winning at Olympia.

Not to be outdone, Gardner, who was raised on a Nebraska dairy farm, grew strong by carrying sick calves on his shoulder and lifting four milk buckets at a time. Karelin was no slouch either. The six-foot-three-inch, 286-pound Siberian once lifted a five-hundred-pound refrigerator off the lobby floor of his apartment building and carried it to his room up eight flights of stairs. So legendary was Karelin's strength that many opponents conceded when they suspected that the end was near, especially when he was about to deploy his "reverse body lift," which meant hoisting and hurling his opponents through the air like rag dolls.

But Gardner was fearless and was not about to be cowed. He stuck to Karelin like human velcro, chest-to-chest, shoulder-to-shoulder with him. The tactic surprised, frustrated, and exhausted his rival. "I knew if I let him push me around," Gardner said, "get even two or three points on me, it was over."

In the middle of the second period, Karelin appeared to lose his concentration for the briefest of moments—just enough time for Gardner to force Karelin's hands apart. The stunning move earned him the first point of the match. Gardner held on to the lead like a man possessed with a vision, until the utterly imaginable happened.

With eight seconds left in regulation time, the man who had not lost in thirteen years of international competition, who was so assured of a record fourth straight gold medal that the president of the IOC, Juan Antonio Samaranch, had come to the arena to hand it to him personally—that very man raised his hand, signaling surrender.

There was a giant gasp of disbelief at the sudden turn of events. David had defeated Goliath. The Washington Senators had beaten those "Damn Yankees." All was suddenly right with the world because anything was possible, which is unofficially part of the Olympic charter.

Then, in dramatic and joyous contrast to all those Olympic athletes who are as tightly wound as an eight-day clock, the exultant Gardner—not knowing what else to do—did a spontaneous backflip on the mat. Immediately, it became the signature move for victorious wrestlers through the rest of the competition.

AN EXCELLENT HOMECOMING

The choreographer of the stirring opening and closing ceremonies at Sydney, Ric Birch, was asked by reporters afterwards about the ceremonies' possible long-term effects. He responded: "A defining moment in Australian history? I'd love to think that the ceremonies will make Australia a better place for the forces of reconciliation, for all the forces of good in society. I'd love to think that would happen. But it's very much up to the audience and, ultimately, ceremonies probably reflect society rather than necessarily create history. What I hope is that it will inspire the people who watched it to move on."

Birch's words invoke the ideal spirit of the Games, which remains a belief in the nobility of fair competition, the merit of personal achievement, and the importance of an approach that addresses the whole person. This ideal reflects the hope that the "values of the game," as ex-senator and Olympian basketball player Bill Bradley calls them, may help athletes become "better prepared for life." Bradley believes that sports can "legitimize youthful aspiration and encourage commitment." But more than vindicating the time, energy, and money invested in sports, Bradley helps us see the bigger picture. "As the ancient Greeks understood," he writes, "great athletes not only accept the ordeal of competition and the trial of strength inherent in it, but also show us a connection between what we do each day and something that is larger than we are and lasts longer than we do."

In the conclusion of his spirit-soaring book, *Values of the Game*, Bradley speculates about the rhythms of the imagination shared by artists, scientists, poets, athletes, and presumably the odd politician:

> For those of us who found it in playing the game, it has shaped our joy in countless ways. It has enriched our experience and

allowed us to feel the thrill of fresh creation. It puts us in touch with what most makes us human. Above all, it enables us to see beyond the moment, to transcend our circumstances however dire they appear, and to reply to the common wisdom that says we cannot soar by saying, "Just watch!"

That is, watch the spirit of excellence that is present in every Olympic tale of courage, determination, passion, optimism, fearlessness, inspiration, and its ability to turn any defeat into victory if we learn something about ourselves. Watch and pay excellent attention to the unexpected details that bring alive the often-hidden meaning in Olympic competition.

This watching is what sportswriter Steve Ruskin was doing when he noticed a curious ritual enacted by tourists who had noticed that the Olympic cauldron was placed so high above the stadium that it was visible even from nearby streets. "A picture snapped from certain angles on Olympic Boulevard made it appear that you were holding it aloft, like Liberty's torch." Holding what? The Olympic cauldron. "All over Olympic Park," he wrote, "[visitors representing] the planet's populace held it high in [their] right hands, in imitation of the Statue of Liberty." With this trick of perspective, the visitors were able to act out the ancient and irrepressible desire to light the sacred torch, to tend the sacred fire.

Again displaying a keen eye for metaphor, Ruskin noticed the first names of some of the competitors that seemed to uncannily express a few of the otherwise ineffable qualities or gifts that are granted to those who are fortunate enough to attend the Games. "About all we'll retain," Ruskin concluded, "when the torch is extinguished, are the names of a few Nigerian athletes: Charity, Patience, Mercy, Gentle, Victor, Blessing."

THE
PHILOSOPHER
COACH

---※---

The Art of
Winning Wisely

Like runners

they hand on the torch of life.

—LUCRETIUS

If an athlete wants to be an Olympic champion,
he must cleave to his destiny, and work hard
until he achieves his goal.

— PERCY CERUTTY,
New Zealand track coach

✳

"By skill, charioteer outpasses charioteer," wise Nestor advises his son in Homer's *Iliad*. "He who has put all his confidence in his horses and chariot and recklessly makes a turn that is loose one way or another finds his horses drifting out of the course and does not control them." This piece of fatherly wisdom is part of a long, poetic set of instructions about the fine art of chariot racing, written by the great blind bard around 700 B.C.E., and is considered the oldest known example of athletic advice. Considering how close this date is to the legendary founding of the Olympic Games, Homer, speaking authoritatively about the athletic activity of his time, could be called the world's first sportswriter.

The scene with Nestor and his son, Antilochus, reveals the back story about early Olympic training. For the first couple of centuries, there were no official training grounds, no gymnasiums, and no professional trainers. Athletes were advised by their fathers, resorted to their own military experience, or simply relied on their common sense and powers of observation while watching other athletes.

But then, as now, athletes were always looking for the ideal training regimen that might earn them a prize. As the prestige and glamour of athletic festivals increased, so did the call for specialization. In the early sixth century B.C.E., a complex of training rooms, baths, open grounds, and temples was constructed at Olympia, and shortly thereafter the first trainers appeared, the earliest mentioned being the one who exhorted the boxer Glaucus to victory at the 520 B.C.E. Games. The Greeks used three different terms for professional trainers. The *paidotribes* were "polishers of boys," referring to their skills as masseurs and athletic drills; *aleiptes* were knowledgeable about hygiene, diet, and physiotherapy; and *gymnastes* were experts in physical literally "nude exercise," nearest to today's coaches. Often the roles were interchangeable, but the goal of all trainers, who were often retired athletes, was to groom the "gilded youth" into champions. The philosopher Antiphon was impressed with how, "training makes athletes as golden—gleaming as the columns in the Palaestra—and solid as stone. Pindar was not above crediting five trainers in his victor odes, calling them *tekton*, "carpenters" or "builders" of athletes. He also commented that to get to the sacred Games, to earn your "heart's desire for glory," you must seek out a master.

So successful were these private trainers that one of them, Iccus, a former Olympic pentathlon champion, collected his advice into a book, published some time after 444 B.C.E. Over the next several centuries, scores of trainers' textbooks, manuals, and even scientific treatises were published, but only a scant few remain.

Then there were the profuse commentaries by philosophers, poets, and politicians—including Plato, Aristotle, Epictetus, and Marcus Aurelius—who, as we have seen, frequented gymnasiums and the wrestling schools called *palaistras* all over Greece. They rubbed elbows with athletes and trainers and mused about the impact of athletics on individual character, citizenship, morals, and overall health. A later writer, Philostratus, author of *Gymnastes*, the most complete ancient text on the subject, argues and debates the moral codes and ethics surrounding the training of athletes for the great prize games. Finley and Pleket report the comment of a young Asia Minor athlete, about 100 B.C.E., that the gymnasiums were centers of training "for the body and the soul."

Over time, the philosophical musings of the intellectuals, officials, trainers, and athletes coalesced into strict moral codes propounded by the athletic complexes and often publicly displayed. In the second century, one such set of laws was posted at the local gymnasium in Verroia, Macedonia. It announced the established guidelines for the gymnasium's publicly elected leader, who oversaw the trainers and other staff. Etched onto a marble stele, or pillar, on exhibit in the gymnasium and *palaistra*, for the clutch of athletes and swarm of spectators it was a daily reminder of the elite standards demanded by the *hellanodikai*— the judges—at Olympia. And for the head trainer it became sacred oath. As translated by Stephen L. Mitchell, the stone reads:

> I swear by Herakles and Hermes that I will be a gymnasiarchos [trainer] in accordance with the gymnasiarchal law, and that I will do anything and everything not covered by the law in the most just manner I possibly can . . . And I will not do any special favors for my friends nor unjust injuries to my enemies; and from existing revenues for the young neither will I myself steal, nor will I allow anyone else to steal in any way that I might know or that I might discover. If I am true to my oath, may all be well with me; if not, may the opposite be my fate.

Remarkably, the stone even declares who wrote the oath: "the *gymnasiarchos* Zopyros, son of Amyntas, Asklepiades son of Heras, and Kallipos son of Hippostratos."

The Verroia stele reveals the ancient Greeks' concern about the shadow side of athletics, which had been on the increase for several centuries, and represents similar monuments passed across the empire. Though the Olympics were regarded as the greatest of all athletic festivals until their demise in 393 C.E., sporadic problems stiffened the resolve of the officials at Elis, and eventually the trainers all over Greece, to maintain the Games' integrity. Under their scrutiny, the trainer was expected to be above reproach in virtually every area of instruction—which included enforcing a strict ethical code. In those days, that meant having the moral strength to resist bribery, theft, and sexual impropriety. The trainer was also expected to remind his charges that besides "seeking fame through pain," as the saying went, they should compete for deeper motives: the pride of their family and homeland, and "the glory of Zeus."

If I am true to my oath, may all be well with me; if not, may the opposite be my fate. This last line of the ancient oath reveals the overall intention of Olympic officials to ensure the Games' religious and ethical codes, as well as the trainer's personal code of honor. If true to his sacred code, he will live nobly; if not, he will suffer disgrace. Hardly sanctimonious, the declaration voices a deeper, philosophical meaning for the trainer's lot in life: building champions for the honor of the gods.

In the oath's sentiments, we can hear the first faint but recognizable voice of the coach who aims to transcend the age-old obsession with victory. We can also make out the early traces of what it means to be a coach with a conscience, a mentor with moral integrity. Clearly, in ancient times, as now, while great athletes were distinguished by their own excellence, great coaches—those we might call philosopher coaches—were those who excelled in their care for the excellence of others.

"In a nutshell"—referring to the early Greek practice of storing nut-sized miniature books inside nutshells—a philosopher coach, like all philosophers, is a lover of wisdom, in this case, the wisdom of the sporting life. He or she—from Zopyros to Knute Rockne—is trainer, teacher, mentor, counselor, parental figure, and soul guide all wrapped into one. The wise coach teaches his or her players what skills they need to improve, yes, but also why the training and the games *matter*. As such, he or she passes along lessons for life, such as loyalty, focus, capacity for discipline, ability to overcome adversity, and willingness to play as part of a team or for a greater cause.

Gary Walton, track coach at the University of California at Davis, calls the coach or trainer who can convey the wisdom of sports—so easily lost in the race for the gold—the modern equivalent of Plato's philosopher king. Such coaches "are like ancient sages," he writes. "They are a special brand of leaders, role models for other coaches and noncoaches alike to follow." Walton is quick to point out that they are not faultless, but they can still "provide sterling quality leadership and examples worth following."

For Walton, one coach who embodies the ancient spirit is the legendary Percy Wells Cerutty. While growing up in Melbourne as an ailing child, Cerutty drove himself to become a highly successful miler, then fell ill again and was unable to train for the 1920 Olympics. In the spirit of ancient shamans, he healed himself through a vigorous physical, mental, and spiritual regimen and, in his mid-fifties, transformed himself once again, this time into a track coach. His Stotan (from Stoic and Spartan) Creed became world famous: *strength through nature*. Citing alike philosophers, poets, and mystics, such as St. Francis of Assisi, Cerutty extolled the mystical virtue of suffering for a higher cause. He often said great runners "must learn to die a little." His unconventional methods, like running without a program, eating only whole foods, and sleeping outside, led to world records for several of his long distance runners, most notably Australian 5,000-meter champion Herb Eliot. Some considered

Cerutty's style fanatical. But he guided his runners not so much by tinkering with their technique as by attending to their inner life—their drives, motivations, and desires.

"I raise the spirits of the athletes," he said, "and inspire the soul to a higher state of consciousness. As the athlete grows spiritually as a person, his performance in the physical will gradually unfold to new heights."

In the 1960 Rome Games, Eliot was the odds-on favorite to win the 5,000 meters. After one lap he passed Frenchman Michel Bernard and took off like "a scared bunny," he later said, because he thought someone was hot on his heels, although he was really off to an easy victory. On the backstretch he caught sight of Coach Cerutty by the side of the track waving a white towel, their old signal that he was on a record-setting pace and should turn on the afterburners. However, this time Cerutty was only excited to see his star runner so far ahead and had forgotten he was not supposed to be near the track. While Cerutty was hauled away by security guards, Eliot, inspired by the sight of his coach and by his own fear that he might still be passed, poured it on and won by a startling twenty yards in the world-record time of 3:35.6.

"The main thing about Percy," Eliot wrote in his autobiography, "is that he coaches your spirit. The body itself may only need two months training to get fit; the rest of the time you're building up your spirit—call it guts, or some inner force—so that it will work for you in a race without your even knowing it."

THE TASK OF TASKS

An Arabian proverb says, "Keep the gold, keep the silver, but give us wisdom." It has long been the job of the philosopher coach, whether on a children's playground or an elder community's tennis courts, to transcend the fleeting moment of the game, winnow the life wisdom from the competition, and then pass that on to his or her athletes.

Such a coach must learn to see through the illusion (from *ludere*, "to play, to mock") of competitive sports as through a looking glass to the other side, where loom deeper truths. The illusion is that winning is the only worthy goal. But rather than getting discouraged about the corrosive effects of the cult of winning, as many parents and people in the antisports movement do, the wise coach recognizes that the illusion is inseparable from the treasure. The dramatic tension inherent in every contest is what pulls us forward. Otherwise, as Bill Bradley once said, athletes get lazy. "The really great [college] coaches," he writes, "engage their players to be best ... Their players may never become pros, but because they learned the values of the game they are better prepared for life."

In his essay, "Can the Joy of Sports Be Saved?" Wilfred Sheed describes an interview with Bill Bradley in which the interviewer asked Bradley if he didn't think the media was out of place in their emphasis on winning, fully expecting the liberal ballplayer and politician to agree. Bradley, however, commented on the downside of players who never bond as teammates and thus never form a team to win. "He said, in effect," writes Sheed, "'No—if you don't emphasize winning over everything else players tend to become selfish.'"

The task of tasks for the philosopher coach is to know when to stress winning and then when to *unstress* it. Recently, I asked a twelve-year veteran of major league baseball, Bruce Bochte, about that vital distinction. He responded:

I definitely agree with those great sages of the games about the pursuit of excellence. Winning is a measurement of excellence. Therefore, when you go to play every day, the great cliché is that winning is the only thing that matters.

And it is undoubtedly the best way to keep the team focused on the goal. But winning is finite. As soon as it is achieved, it is over. It is in the past. Great to hang your hat on. As a culture we have an obsession with it. But transcending winning is a lifelong pursuit of excellence. That is infinite, or at least surpasses our temporal and limited abilities, always beckoning us further and further into the future. Winning is a unique combination of excellence and contingency (being in the right place with the right team at the right time). But the pursuit of excellence is for everyone at all times in every situation.

The philosopher coach's task is to help each player discover the magical balance between playing in the moment and playing *momentously*, that is, in a way that has far-reaching consequences. The results may not appear on the scoreboard, in the box score, or in the record books. But again, as the sign in Einstein's office said, "Not everything that can be counted counts, and not everything that counts can be counted."

What counts, as basketball coach John Wooden often says, is not just what we've won but what we can take with us into the rest of our lives. "Success is never final," he says, "failure is never final. It's courage that counts . . . and what lasts is what you've learned."

What matters to Sheryl Johnson, women's field hockey coach for Stanford University for eighteen years and coach of the gold-medal-winning U.S. team in the 2000 Sydney Games, are the intangibles that will never appear in record books. Stanford's athletic director, Ted Leland, believes her contribution transcends the championships she has won: "She has developed exemplary students, skilled athletes, and model citizens." In Johnson's own words, "Happiness is found along the way, not at the end of the road. People will soon forget the records. What they remember is the way you hustled, the poise you had, the class you showed."

Uncannily, an echo of the ancient Olympic trainer's oath is displayed today in the form of a plaque on the wall of an old Philadelphia sports arena named, coincidentally, the Palestra. It reads:

> To play the game is great,
> To win the game is greater,
> To love the game is the greatest of all.

WHY VICTORY HAS WINGS

The ancient Greeks relished victory, worshipped champions, and immortalized their athletic heroes as much as any modern culture does. And they must have been as stymied as we are today about the seemingly insatiable human longing for winning—and the inevitable melancholy that follows when the ecstasy of having won wears off.

These powerful forces were personified in the mythic figure of Nike, goddess of victory. As depicted in poetry, art, and sculpture, Nike is the angelic messenger who delivers the prized laurel wreath from the true sources of victory, Zeus and Athena, the gods of power and wisdom. The image illustrates the Greek conviction that champions are not born but chosen by the gods—exactly as Sydney Mills described the mysterious scenario to his son, future Olympic champion Billy Mills.

But there is a catch. Nike is winged, as in the famous Winged Victory of Samothrace, now at the Louvre. Her wings are not incidental; they reveal her true nature, which is fleeting

*The bittersweet
pursuit of victory in
the ancient Greek world
was expressed in the saying,
"Wreath—or death!" and in
images of the goddess, Nike, the
winged and forever fleeting messenger.
She is depicted in this frieze fragment, from
Ephesus, Turkey, with the crown of laurels in her
hands as about to crown and immortalize the champion.*

and flirtatious. Nike bears not only the news of victory but also the news that victory does not last long. She keeps moving on to the next contest, the next war, the next champion, forever teasing the warrior, athlete, and poet with the promise of fame. Her name has become synonymous with winning, which is usually felt as a *thrill* and a *swoosh*—the waves of wonderful emotion victory brings in its wake. But that is only half of her power. She also represents the *transience* of triumph, the evanescence of fame, the impermanence of the talent for which victors are often so handsomely rewarded. Her constantly beating wings exist for good reason; they are meant to *move us* beyond our obsession with literal victory, to move us to ponder her deeper message. It is the philosopher coach's task to decipher what that message might be.

THE WISDOM OF DESIRE

At the 1992 Barcelona Games, the preeminent runner for Great Britain, Derek Redmond, was running in the semi-finals heat of the 400 meters when he heard a strange pop from his right leg. He had torn his hamstring, and the sudden explosion of pain turned him into a rag doll. Redmond, the British record holder in the event, collapsed and lay unmoving on the track while the other seven runners completed the race. Never one to quit, Redmond staggered to his feet and began to hobble down the track towards the finish line.

"Suddenly a man appeared on the track," writes Bud Greenspan, "hurrying to the injured runner. He ran past medics who were carrying a stretcher. It was Jim Redmond, trying to catch up to his son. Finally, Jim Redmond reached his son trying to finish the race."

When Redmond reached him, he put his arms around his hobbling son and said, "Look, you don't have to do this." Contorted in pain but utterly determined, Derek Redmond gritted his teeth and replied, "Yes, I do." His father was equally determined, and replied, "Well, if you're going to finish this race, we'll finish it together."

"There, at the Barcelona Olympic stadium," Greenspan continues, "unfolded one of the most memorable scenes in the history of the Olympic Games: a son being helped by his father making their way around the track to the finish line. And in defeat gaining as much glory as if he had won."

The devastating injury cut short Derek Redmond's running career. But he transformed the agony and disappointment into a stellar life as a track and field coach, basketball and rugby player, and motivational speaker. His talks center on "what it takes to persevere, overcome obstacles, and succeed as an individual and as a team."

Not all people have parents they can lean on, as Derek Redmond does; not many of us have someone who will bolster us as we hobble to the finish line of our toughest endeavors. That is why the coach, trainer, teacher, instructor, or mentor is a critical part of everyone's journey.

No one takes an odyssey alone.

THE MENTOR

My high school track coach, Mr. Natkowski, was devoted to his players, a tough disciplinarian but someone who saw the bigger picture. He began the first practice of my freshman season by assembling us on the wooden bleachers inside the gym at Wayne St. Mary's, the local Catholic high school, and telling us not to worry about razzing from players on the school's championship football and basketball teams just because the track team hadn't won a meet in many years. If we just took it one meet at a time, we too could be champions.

In the tradition of other coaches, like John Wooden or Percy Cerutty, who favor sharing the occasional verse with their players, Mr. Nat passed out mimeographed copies of an anonymous poem and read it out loud for us:

> Life's battles don't always go
> To the stronger or faster man,
> But sooner or later, the man who wins
> Is the fellow who thinks he can.

Then he told us something I have never forgotten. "I can make you guys fast runners," he said, his voice trembling with emotion. "I can show you how to throw the shot put, pole vault, and high jump. But that's not really why I am here. I'm here to show you how to become *men*."

For a long time we thought that meant learning how to suffer, though we didn't quite know why. Then I discovered comedian Bill Cosby's hilarious late-1960s record album, *Sports,* where he asks the immortal question that all runners sooner or later ask themselves: "Why do we run around in circles just to make ourselves *throw up?*" Cosby's pitch-perfect impersonation of adolescent angst has come to mind in the middle of many a long run or ballgame since then, usually just when I am wondering, *Why am I doing this?* I've often recalled that lazy Michigan spring afternoon after one particularly grueling track practice when I played the record for several guys on my high school team. When Cosby whined about the agonies of training hard, we all tumbled to the floor laughing until our sides hurt—from the pain of recognition, I suppose.

"Hey, he's right, we must be out of our minds!" shouted my buddy Ryan Sexton, one of our superb long distance runners who later ran a 4:07 mile in college. "We're crazy! What are we trying to prove?" And then his voice dropped like a shot put, his face because serious, and he said what we'd all been thinking: "We're doing it for Mr. Nat. We're trying to prove ourselves to him."

The way Mr. Nat had pronounced the word *men* reverberated with ancient tones of fate and destiny, but it also showed us that he cared. None of us on that team, which went on to win the league championship our senior year, have ever forgotten his devotion.

In September 2001, when I was on a book tour for *Once and Future Myths,* Mr. Nat appeared at Shaman's Drum Bookstore in Ann Arbor, Michigan, where I was giving a reading. In his honor, I read from the chapter on the venerable tradition of mentorship, which features a long passage about his influence on me.

Afterwards, we gathered outside with a few of my ex-teammates, and he growled that his neighbors had nicknamed him

"Mr. Mentor" because of the story in the book. But then he confided something I had never known about him. During my sophomore year, in 1968, he technically couldn't coach our practices due to budgetary problems at the school, though he could lead us at our meets. Nevertheless, he still drove several miles across town every day to post our workouts on the locker room bulletin board. Occasionally, his assistant coach, Gerry Higgs, came around to help us, but we were generally on our own, guided only by Mr. Nat's posted workouts and his constant reminders that we had to be self-motivated. What we didn't know was that Mr. Nat checked up on us several times a week for at least a few minutes from the secrecy of his old black Ford Fairlane. We never saw him, but he could see whether or not we were working out.

"All year long," he told me outside the bookstore, "I kept bumping into Bill Hawley—you remember him, the Wayne High track coach who was holding workouts with his own boys? And he kept telling me he couldn't believe you guys never missed a workout, never slacked off, but all practiced as hard as if I had actually been there on the track, blowing my fool whistle to keep you going.

"Do you know something, Cousineau? I just ran into Hawley recently, and he asked me again—after *thirty years*—what my secret was. 'How did you keep them going without you being there?' He said he didn't believe for a moment his own team would've worked out without him around. I had to tell him I didn't know. Why? Why didn't you guys slack off?"

Mr. Nat's head tilted to the side as he asked me to clear up the old mystery, reminding me of the way he used to ask us questions during practices or meets. Then his eyes began to well with tears of pride.

As the late evening autumn air stirred, I thought of all the night runs and winter workouts on snowbound roads. *Discipline,*

I thought, *discipline, discipline. That was your greatest gift to us. That's why we would've run through brick walls for you.*

"Hey, coach," I suddenly blurted out, "we did it because we loved you. We knew you cared." I surprised myself with the admission but went on anyway, a little choked up, and then tried to lighten things up, as if we were right back in the locker room circa 1968. "I also think we knew you'd be able to tell if we were goofing off. You would have known by our times at the meets, right?"

A smile soared across Mr. Nat's face. He nodded warmly and shook his head in wonder. Then he rattled off a few of our times, our record-setting mile relay time, my own best 440-yard dash and best long jump, plus the best mile, half-mile, and shot put toss by my old teammates. After more than thirty years, he still knew many of our stats by heart.

It was only high school track, a long, long way from the Olympics, but those were Olympic *lessons* he gave us—lessons that had survived the ages, like the athlete statues buried under twenty feet of river silt or hundreds of feet of water. Lessons that last a lifetime, many lifetimes.

"You're always running against your own best," Mr. Nat used to urge us. "Just try to beat your best. Give me your best."

BEING WORTHY

On the morning of the procession from Elis to Olympia, the athletes gathered on the grounds where they had been training for a grueling month. Their trainers then told them, "If you have worked so as to be worthy of going to Olympia, if you have done nothing indolent nor ignoble, then take heart and march on; but those who have not so trained may leave and go wherever they like." Similarly, on the morning of the competitions at Delphi and Corinth, trainers instructed their competing athletes to "Go now into the stadium and be men worthy of winning."

Today the word *worthy* is rarely used in conjunction with the word *winning*. Yet it is often implied, especially when a euphemism like *deserves* is used instead. She *deserved* to win because she tried so hard, or, he *didn't deserve* to win because of his bad attitude or because he was on steroids. The idea of worth, referring to value, honor, and importance, is at the heart of the philosopher coach's creed. But are we *worthy* of winning?

To make athletes of *every* caliber, from benchwarmer to superstar, worthy of winning is the task of the philosopher coach. This calls for a redefinition of what it means to win—which begins with reminding players what it means when they are exhorted or *expected* to win. On the surface, to win means to surpass others; in the depths, to win means to *strive*, and to strive well. "To strive, to seek, and not to yield," say Alfred Lord Tennyson's immortal words about the courage of King Arthur. Whoever strives valiantly, according to both poets and philosopher coaches, is by definition a winner.

But in a culture addicted to the drug of success, anything less than complete victory is twisted into meaning ignominy and *worthlessness*. The greatest task the philosopher coach faces is to turn around this concept of worthlessness so his or her players can appreciate winning for what it is: any form of positive feedback for their best efforts.

Brutus Hamilton, the legendary track and field coach at the University of California at Berkeley, was head coach of the American track team at the 1952 Helsinki Games. In a letter written from London after the Games, he described "the gist" of what his pep talks to his team had been, before they went on to win twenty-two medals: "Honor yourselves, your country, and your opponents with your very best performances and with your very best behavior. I'm certain you shall, for you are already well coached and your parents have already taught you right from wrong. You are a grand group of young men and we coaches expect this to prove the easiest coaching job of our lives." The letter continues: "It proved to be so; so again, I repeat, don't give me undue credit."

As Coach Walton writes in his wonderful essay about Hamilton, "Sport to Brutus was an important extension of humanity, and the best of athletic competition, he felt, was in the ideal of competing for the joy of it." Hamilton aimed to motivate his athletes to work hard and dedicate themselves to a worthwhile goal with enthusiasm, will, and determination. And the fastest way to get there was learning to run purely, but with passion. "Running," he was fond of saying, "is clean and noble."

RADICALLY
REDEFINING SUCCESS

According to H. A. Harris, the ancient Olympic Games were "an integrated preparation for a life of quality." This transcendent form of training for success in life, not just in sports, is the secret strength of our philosopher coaches today, like Susan Jackson, Charles Riley, Percy Cerutty, and legendary basketball coach John Wooden.

"Players fifty years ago wanted to win just as much as players today," writes Wooden. "Foot soldiers a thousand years ago wanted to win the battle as much as combat troops today. Athletes today have no greater desire to win than athletes at the first Olympic Games. The desire then and now is the same . . . In classical times, the courageous struggle for a noble cause was considered success in itself. Sadly, that ideal has been forgotten. But it is well worth remembering."

According to the dictionary, *success* means "a favorable or desired outcome." In common usage it refers to the attainment of wealth or fame, and in the sporting world, to winning—and winning *large*, as they say today, meaning championships. By any standard, John Wooden was one of the most successful coaches of the twentieth century, having led his UCLA basketball team to ten national championships in twelve years. More impressive, however, is that his eye was always on the greater prize. Winning was never as important to him as the challenge of instilling in his players a revolutionary—for our time—reappraisal of success and a soulful emphasis on doing one's absolute best.

Coach Wooden bases his famous approach on the simple principles he inherited from his father, growing up as a boy on a small Indiana farm. First on the list was: "Be true to yourself." Second was: "Help others." His commonsense philosophy made him seem unfashionable in his early years as a teacher and coach, but it set the stage for the stellar career that followed.

In his 1984 videotape, *Pyramid of Success,* Wooden says, "Long ago I wasn't satisfied with what was generally considered to be success, which was the accumulation of material possessions or the attainment of a position of power or prestige. I don't think those things necessarily indicate success, but they might. So after a lot of thinking, I came up with my own definition." His belief and his practice point to what he feels is vital to living a good life: "a higher standard of success than merely winning." This standard is a blend of common sense, old world values, and a dash of what one of his star pupils, Kareem Abdul-Jabbar, calls Wooden's "mystic quality."

"Success," says John Wooden, "is peace of mind attained only through self-satisfaction in knowing you've made the effort to do the best of which you're capable." With characteristic honesty, Wooden confesses that when people ask him if he has lived up to his own model of the Pyramid of Success, "My answer is always the same: No. But I've tried."

Wooden's coaching philosophy is in line with the wisdom voiced by a plethora of thinkers throughout history. Ralph Waldo Emerson, for instance, said, "Wisdom comes more from the heart than from the head." William Faulkner advised, "Don't bother to be better than your contemporaries or predecessors. Try to be better than yourself." Wooden often echoed him in telling his players, "Never try to be better than anyone else, but be the best *you* can be."

The depth of Coach Wooden's conviction about taking pride in one's own personal best causes him to worry about the modern Olympics. "I no longer feel that supportive of the Olympic Games, which have become almost professional," he writes in his recent book, *Wooden*. "You'll see an athlete complaining about coming in second because he knows it will cost him in endorsements. Going for the gold has too often become going for the green." Instead, Wooden says, the right question in sports, as in life, is: "Did I make my best effort? That's what matters. The rest of it just gets in the way."

FROM JOYLESS PLAY
TO FAIR PLAY

David C. Young writes, "The fundamental Greek view of the aim of athletics was to gain the satisfaction of victory and a sense of physical well-being in return for hardship, exhaustion, and discomfort."

No doubt, the satisfaction and pride of victory can inspire the virtues of hard work. A healthy winning attitude can help prepare athletes, and even fans, to deal with the tough realities of the ultracompetitive modern world. A ferocious drive to win may also work as a safety valve for young people's aggressive behavior. But what happens when the stress on winning transmogrifies into the monstrous demand to win at all costs?

In *The Sports Medicine Book*, Gabe Mirkin reports that he polled over one hundred elite runners about whether or not they would take a magic elixir he called the "Olympic Pill," if they knew it would transform them into Olympic champions—even though they would die a year later.

More than half said yes.

Likewise, in Michael Clarkson's *Competitive Fire*, sports advisor John Douillard says, "Second place means nothing these days, especially with so much riding on victory—trophies, earnings, corporate sponsors, and self-esteem. We've put so much pressure on winning, we've traded in the process of getting there, the enjoyment process of sports which many athletes these days never achieve. The fun has gone out of it."

Gary Walton explains the source of the gale-force winds of commerce and cynicism that a well-meaning coach is up against: "The special virtues and characteristics of the philosopher coach are being smothered by the new, additional talents needed to win and promote the game. No one is to blame. It is not the fault of the coaches, nor the players, team owners, or fans. The changing character of coaching is being driven by the market place, by the growing number of fans willing and able to pay top dollar for sports entertainment, by technical progress in the development of athletes, and by the media."

When the Olympic ideal of struggling and participation is defamed, the addiction to perfection can take over. Its influence ripples out across the entire culture, as evidenced by the disturbing disclosure that more and more kids are dropping out of organized sports. At least 75 percent of kids stop playing by age twelve, according to Scott Lancaster in his revolutionary book, *Fair Play*. And the reasons range from boredom to shame to too little playing time, poor teaching, not enough learning or improving, too much focus on winning, and hardly any joy.

Fair enough, says the "fair play" movement. In the beginning, we will encourage kids to play for the sake of play and no more. No score, no points, and no winners. In real play, we will remind them, there is no goal and no prize.

So far, the fair play model seems to be working. Coaches and parents across the country report growing enthusiasm for participation in sports among school-age kids. Nevertheless, there is another level of engagement in sports that leads inexorably to higher forms of competition, to games where the only object is to win, to conquer, to gain advantage.

Many modern coaches believe there is a connection between the terrific pressure to win at the most elite levels, from the major leagues to the Olympics, and the joyless and businesslike approach that now pervades our sports. Those who care about the current and future health of all of our games, culminating in the Olympics, do not deny the value of competition, nor do they wish to suppress the joy that accompanies victory. Instead, they ask for a more mythopoetic approach to sports—less talk about money and more talk about beauty, less obsession about celebrities and more focus on sportsmanship, excellence, humility, and the spirit-lifting power of personal bests. This caliber of coach speaks up for, and stands for, qualities that allow the entire community to grow stronger.

One such coach is Steve Glass, former player in the Atlanta Braves organization and now athletic director and award-winning teacher and coach at Cathedral School for Boys in San Francisco. Coach Glass told me in a recent interview that his philosophy is to teach his kids how to compete and win—with perspective, especially in light of the often unrealistic expectations thrust upon them.

"I see my role as coach as going behind the x's and o's," he told me, "to teach them life lessons, like developing good qualities as human beings, such as trust, honesty, sportsmanship, and integrity. These characteristics are much more important than the outcome of one random game. As long as my students are having fun, giving their best effort, and never giving up, they are winners no matter the outcome. If they understand that, then I have done my job."

When I asked Glass about the Olympics' influence on him and his aspiring athletes, his response was impassioned: "The Olympics have incredible value to me as a teacher and a coach," he said. "Sports teach kids the value of making friends, how to deal effectively with adversity, the importance of getting along with teammates, fundamental skills, and a healthy lifestyle. Olympic athletes are incredible role models for kids in terms of their commitment, hard work, and dedication. They provide a kind of ideal to offer them that I just can't find anywhere else, in college or pro sports. The Olympic ideal was founded on a belief that countries could come together in the spirit of competition; the outcome would be secondary . . . No matter their country, every kid in the world can appreciate an outstanding athletic performance, and the Olympics provide the grandest stage."

Our inspiring interview transported me back to the playing days of my own youth, when the gods graced me with coaches who were both wise teachers and tough trainers. They helped me, in the ancient tradition of the mentor, to "make up my own mind," which meant, in the language of sports, find my swing, pace myself, groove my shot. I thought of Coach McCaffrey, my firebrand Irish baseball coach, who told us before a championship game, "To hell with all that stuff about sports *building* character—it *reveals* character. Now get your *characters* out on the field and win this thing!" I remembered the humbling words of Ron Gold, basketball coach for the club team I played for in London in the mid-seventies, seconds after the buzzer sounded on my finest game of the season (44 points, 19 rebounds) and our most resounding victory, over a team from the nearby U.S. Air Force base. At the height of our euphoria in the post-game huddle, he reminded us of what James Naismith, the Canadian inventor of basketball, used to tell his players: "Let us all be able to lose graciously and to win courteously; to accept criticism as well as praise; and last of all, to appreciate the attitude of the other fellow at all times." Then he led us across court to shake hands with our opponents. I vividly remember the strong emotions that rose up in me and the utter surprise on their faces as we looked each in the eye and thanked them for a great game.

Olympic lessons abound concerning the ties that bind together philosopher coaches and their athletes. Of all the fabled relationships, perhaps the most storied and inspiring is that of Jesse Owens and his coach, an Irishman named Charles Riley. Riley was so convinced he had detected something special in Owens that he rose every morning at dawn to train him before they both had to appear at school. Rather than training hard to reach what Owens thought what his limit, Riley taught him to push past that border to the mysterious place where victory is always found. What Owens learned to appreciate in his coach was that, "Somehow, Mr. Riley had found the secret of winning that victory anew for himself each day, and for helping others to win it." Owens credits his own ability to transcend the terrific pressure he was under at the Berlin Games to his beloved coach, for Riley had taught him well that he wasn't competing against any other athlete or even against another nation.

"As I'd learned long ago from Charles Riley," he wrote later, "the only victory that counts is the one over yourself."

Owens learned something else from his coach, as the film version of his life portrays—something that comes not from running but from slowing down to a saunter and listening. "If we walk long enough," Riley says to Owens in the movie, "and talk long enough, we might get to understand one another."

RECLAIMING THE GAMES

Every two years, I marvel as thousands of athletes gather to compete at the next round of the summer or winter Olympic Games. My mind still runs wild, my heart races, and I feel nearly as exultant and free as I did when I ran a hundred miles a week, or played basketball five hours a day. I have come to see the four sides of the television, the four edges of the newspaper, or the four walls of the stadium, which simultaneously encapsulate and convey to me the action of the Games, as the ancient Persians viewed their walled gardens, their *pairidaeza*—as "paradise." For it is in paradise that we finally return home. It is there that we catch a glimpse of our better selves; it is there that our spirits finally roam free.

I believe this is one reason why the Olympic Games remain as relevant as ever: they continue to carry us away from our daily troubles and *tran-sport* us to the closed garden of the gods. As A. Bart Giamatti writes in his inspired essay on our glorious love of all great games:

> All play aspires to the condition of paradise. It is the condition of freedom that paradise signals, and that play or sport—however hedged in by the world—wishes to mirror, however fleetingly . . . So games, contests, sports reiterate the purpose of freedom every time they are enacted, the purpose being to show how to be free and to be complete and connected, unimpeded and integrated, all at once. That is the role of leisure, and if leisure were a god, rather than Aristotle's version of the highest human state, sport would be a constant reminder—not a faded remnant—of that transcendent or sacred being . . . As our forebears did, we remind ourselves through sport of what, here on earth, is our noblest hope. Through sport, we re-create our daily portion of freedom, in public.

The Olympic Games teach us that life can be a festival, that competitions can enliven the entire community, that the desire to excel makes winners of us all, and that playing at the meaning of life is a noble thing. To convey the spirit of the ancient Games and the soul of the modern Games to the next generation is now our hope; to pass the torch of our passion for a life of excellence is now our task.

Carl Lewis won ten medals in four Olympics from 1984 to 1996.
He hopes his greatest legacy is in showing young people
that there are no limits to our dreams.

EPILOGUE

AN OLYMPIC VISION
FOR THE FUTURE

*I have run the great race,
I have finished the course.
I have kept the faith.*

—St. Paul

The ball once struck off.

Away flies the boy

To the next destined post.

And then home with joy.

—Anonymous (1774)

———————— ✳ ————————

Since the first foot race at Olympia nearly twenty-eight hundred years ago, the Great Games have dramatized the essential life struggle of overcoming ordeals with courage, strength, and grace. At their best, they transform that struggle into sublime performance art—passion plays that reveal our longing for miracles, redemption, and glimpses of perfection.

The unswerving idealism of the Olympic movement still serves an indispensable function, but it is one that transcends its obvious place as a showcase for elite competition. Its transcendent purpose is to remind us that, as tragic as life may be, "You must praise the mutilated world," in the startling words of poet Adam Zagjaweski. These words are not far in tone from that of perhaps the greatest Olympian of all, Jesse Owens. The wisdom he brought home from the 1936 Berlin Games, he concluded, was that, "What makes life bearable is what is higher."

Even in the most dispirited of times, the Olympic Games have proved themselves worthy of our respect moment by incandescent moment. We have learned to lean on them much as the British runner Derek Redmond leaned on his father's shoulder—

to gain a *frisson* of what it feels like to have something in common with the rest of the world. In this sense the Olympics fulfill the ancient dream of having a shared purpose—an *odyssey*—we can all appreciate. This is why gold medal winner Matt Biondi advises young athletes: "Enjoy the journey, enjoy the moment, and quit worrying about winning and losing." And in this shared purpose, *praise* is the mysterious force that restores the spirit, rekindles the fire and passes the torch, and helps us find our way home again.

In the spirit of the ancient trainers who posted their sacred oaths, or of the philosophers and aspiring athletes who posted victor lists on gymnasia walls, I have compiled a few lists to photocopy and hang in the locker room or on a bulletin board at home. They are intended solely to remind young athletes, coaches, parents, spectators, and media mavens about the holy fire in the heart of sports that is dying to be rekindled.

NINE SUGGESTIONS TO REKINDLE THE SPIRIT OF THE GAMES

1. Revive the sacred dimension by emphasizing ritual, ceremony, and storytelling, such as retelling the origins of the ancient festival, as well as the origins of each event.

2. Restore the ancient emphasis on beauty and philosophy, in contrast to the modern mania about statistics and medals, by inviting artists, poets, and intellectuals to add their commentary to that of the usual sports experts and ex-athletes.

3. Re-vision the ancient tradition of competition in drama, oratory, poetry, and history with an updated version of those contests, including film and video.

4. Renew the attention the ancient Greeks gave to the ideal of mind, body, and spirit with a special award to an athlete who embodies an all-around integration.

5. Review the post-Olympic lives of the alumni, in radio and television interviews, so that more people know how athletes may share their experience and wisdom with others. Examples include Muhammad Ali's youth programs in Louisville, Kentucky, or the motivational speeches and coaching of Nadia Comaneci and her husband Bart Conner.

6. Reward the wise ways of a philosopher coach with a tribute to the merits of healthy, innovative, and compassionate training.

7. Review the U.S. Olympic Spirit Award so that it is paid proper attention during and after the Games, and institute a Spirit Award for the athlete who overcame the most adversity to participate—but not necessarily win a medal—in the Games.

8. Represent the effect that peaceful competition had on the English silver medalist Philip Baker, who later won the Nobel Peace Prize, with an International Peace-keeping Award for the athlete contributing the most to world peace.

9. Rekindle the ancient tradition of the Olympic Peace Truce—which suspended all wars for the Games' duration—by sending official heralds to the capital of each nation around the world. These heralds, in announcing the next Olympiad, shall remind each nation of the age-old Olympic dream of fostering brotherhood and peace.

THE U.S. OLYMPIC SPIRIT
AWARD WINNERS' LIST

The U.S. Olympic Spirit Award recognizes American athletes who best exemplify the spirit of Olympic competition through courage, dedication, and determination in overcoming adversity while achieving their Olympic goal and inspiring others to follow their dream. The athletes are nominated by a panel of ten U.S. Olympic Alumni. Criteria for the award are *Perseverance*, the capacity to pursue a goal after having encountered adversity; *Commitment*, the long-term dedication to goals; *Courage*, the inner strength to overcome apparently impossible situations; and *Vision*, the ability to focus on a goal regardless of obstacles.

Year	Summer Games	Winter Games
2002		Chris Klug, *Snowboard* Vonetta Flowers and Jill Bakken, *Bobsled*
2000	Rulon Gardner, *Wrestling* Laura Wilkinson, *Diving*	
1996	Kerri Strug, *Gymnastics* Carl Lewis, *Track and Field*	
1992	Gail Devers, *Track and Field*	Paul Wylie, *Figure Skating*
1988	Greg Louganis, *Diving*	Dan Jansen, *Speed Skating*
1994	Jeff Blatnick, *Wrestling*	Scott Hamilton, *Figure Skating*
1980	Tracy Caulkins, *Swimming*	Tai Babilonia and Randy Gardner, *Pairs Skating*
1976	Margaret Murdock, *Shooting*	Andy Mill, *Downhill Skiing*
1972	Dave Wottle, *Track and Field*	Mike Curran, *Ice Hockey*
1968	Bob Beamon, *Track and Field*	Billy Kidd, *Downhill Skating*

THE TEN COMMANDMENTS OF TRUE SPORTSMANSHIP

(adapted from H. A. Harris's *How Did Sports Begin?*)

Thou shalt not quit.

Thou shalt not alibi.

Thou shalt not gloat over winning.

Thou shalt not sulk over losing.

Thou shalt not take unfair advantage.

Thou shalt not ask odds thou art unwilling to give.

Thou shalt always give opponents the benefit of a doubt.

Thou shalt not underestimate an opponent or overestimate thyself.

Thou shalt remember that the game is the thing and not the athlete.

Thou shalt honor the game that thou playest, for he who plays straight wins even when he loses.

COACH JOHN WOODEN'S EIGHT SUGGESTIONS FOR SUCCEEDING

- Fear no opponent. *Respect* every opponent.

- Remember, it's the perfection of the smallest details that make big things happen.

- Keep in mind that hustle makes up for a mistake.

- Be more interested in character than reputation.

- Be quick, but don't hurry.

- Understand that the harder you work, the more luck you will have.

- Know that valid self-analysis is crucial for improvement.

- Remember that there is no substitute for hard work and careful planning. Failing to prepare is preparing to fail.

COACH LEONARD NATKOWSKI'S HAND-OUT

If you think you are beaten, you are.
If you think that you dare not, you don't.
If you'd like to win, but you think you can't,
It's almost certain you won't.

If you think you'll lose, you've lost,
For out in the world you'll find
Success begins with a fellow's will.
It's all in the state of mind.

Life's battles don't always go
To the stronger or faster man;
But sooner or later the man who wins
Is the man who thinks he can.

—ANONYMOUS

TWELVE GREAT LINES ABOUT
FLEET-FOOTED VICTORY

A Shropshire Lad

The time you won your town the race
We chaired you through the market-place;
Man and boy stood cheering by,
And home we brought you shoulder-high.
Smart lad, to slip betimes away
From fields where glory does not stay
And early though the laurel grows
It withers quicker than the rose.
Now you will not swell the rout
Of lads that wore their honors out,
Runners whom renown outran
And the name died before the man.

—A. E. Housman

*Everything here is a game
A passing thing,
What matters is what I've done
And what I'll leave behind,
Let it be an example
For those that come.*

—Pele
Brazilian soccer star

RECOMMENDED READING

———————— ✳ ————————

Anderson, Dave. *The Story of the Olympics*. New York: HarperCollins, 2000.

Andronicos, Manolis. *Olympia*. Athens: Ekdotike Athenon, 1982.

Arlott, John. *Pageantry of Sport*. New York: Hawthorn Books, 1968.

Baker, William J. *Sports in the Western World*. Totowa, N.J.: Rowman and Littlefield, 1982.

Barney, Robert K., Stephen R. Wenn, and Scott G. Martyn. *Selling Five Rings: The International Olympic Committee and the Rise of Olympic Commericialism*. Salt Lake City: University of Utah Press, 2002.

Bradley, Bill. *Values of the Game*. New York: Broadway Books, 1998.

Brasch, R. *How Did Sports Begin? A Look at the Origins of Man at Play*. New York: David McKay, 1970.

Coubertin, Pierre de. *Olympic Memoirs*. Rev. ed. Lausanne: International Olympic Committee, 1979.

Dickinson, G. Lowes. *The Greek View of Life*. Chautauqua, N.Y.: Chautauqua Press, 1909.

Drees, Ludwig. *Olympia: Gods, Artists, and Athletes*. New York and Washington: Frederick A. Praeger, 1968.

Ecker, Tom. *Olympic Facts and Fables*. Mountain View, Calif.: Tafnews Press, 1996.

Epictetus. *The Art of Living: The Classic Manual on Virtue, Happiness, and Effectiveness*. Versions by Sharon Lobell. San Francisco: HarperSanFrancisco, 1994.

Gardner, E. Norman. *Athletics of the Ancient World*. Chicago: Ares Publishers, 1930.

Giamatti, A. Bartlett. *Take Time for Paradise: Americans and Their Games*. New York: Summit Books, 1989.

Halberstam, David, ed. *The Best American Sports Writing of the Century*. New York and Boston: Houghton Mifflin, 1999.

Hamill, Sam, ed. *The Infinite Moment: Poems from Ancient Greek*. New York: New Directions Books, 1992.

Harris, H. A. *Greek Athletes and Athletics*. Bloomington and London: Indiana University Press, 1966.

————. *Sport in Greece and Rome: Aspects of Greek and Roman Life*. Ithaca, N.Y.: Cornell University Press, 1972.

Harrison, Jane. *Themis: A Study of the Social Origins of Greek Religion*. London: Merlin Press, 1963.

Heinrich, Bernd. *Why We Run: A Natural History* (originally published as *Racing the Antelope: What Animals Can Teach Us about Running and Life*) New York: HarperCollins, 2001.

Holmes, Burton. *The Olympic Games in Athens, 1896: The First Modern Olympics*. New York: Grove Press, 1994.

Huizinga, Johann. *Homo Ludens*. New York: Harper & Row, 1970.

Leonard, George. *The Ultimate Athlete*. Berkeley, Calif.: North Atlanta Books, 2001.

Miller, David L. *Gods and Games: Toward a Theology of Play*. New York and Cleveland: World Publishing, 1969.

Miller, Stephen G. *Arete: Greek Sports from Ancient Sources*. Berkeley: University of California Press, 1991.

Mogulof, Milly. *Foiled: Hitler's Jewish Olympian*. Oakland, Calif.: RDR Books, 2002.

Murphy, Michael, and Rhea White. *In the Zone: Transcendent Experience in Sports*. New York: Penguin Arkana, 1995.

Nabakov, Peter. *Indian Running*. Santa Barbara, Calif.: Capra, 1981.

Nicholson, Shirley J. *The Seven Human Powers*. Wheaton, Ill.: Quest Books, 2003.

Novak, Michael. *The Joy of Sports*. New York: Harper Colophon, 1976.

Owens, Jesse, with Paul Neimark. *Jesse: A Spiritual Autobiography*. Plainfield, N.J.: Logos International, 1978.

Pausanius. *Descriptions of Greece, Books I-II, III-IV*. Trans. W. H. S. Jones. Cambridge, Mass. and London: Harvard University Press, 1918.

Pele, with Robert L. Fish. *Pele: My Life and the Beautiful Game*. Garden City, N.Y.: Doubleday, 1977.

Pindar. *Olympian Odes, Pythian Odes.* Ed. and trans. William H. Race. Cambridge, Mass. and London: Harvard University Press, 1997.

Read, Sir Herbert. *The Art of Sculpture.* Princeton, N.J.: Bollingen Press, 1956.

Rexroth, Kenneth, trans. *Poems from the Greek Anthology: Expanded Edition.* Ann Arbor, Mich.: University of Michigan Press, 1999.

Ritter, Lawrence S. *The Glory of Their Times: The Story of the Early Days of Baseball Told by the Men Who Played It.* New York: Quill/William Morrow, 1992.

Sheed, Willard. "Can the Joy of Sports Be Saved?" The Wilson Quarterly, vol. xix, no. 1 (winter, 1995).

Silverman, Al. *It's Not Over 'Til It's Over: The Stories behind the Most Magnificent Heart-Stopping Sports Miracles of Our Time.* Woodstock and New York: Overlook Books, 2002.

Swaddling, Judith. *The Ancient Olympic Games.* London: British Museum Press, 1980.

Toms, Michael. *An Open Life: Joseph Campbell in Conversation with Michael Toms.* Comp. and ed. John M. Maher and Dennie Briggs. New York: Larson Publications, 1988.

Van der Leeuw, Gerardus. *Sacred and Profane Beauty: The Holy in Art.* New York: Holt, Rinehart and Winston, 1963.

Walton, Gary M. *Beyond Winning: The Timeless Wisdom of Great Philosopher Coaches.* Champaign, Ill.: Leisure Books, 1992.

Weissmuller, Johnny, Jr., with William Reed and W. Craig Reed. *Tarzan: My Father.* Toronto: ECW Press, 2002.

Wooden, John, with Steve Jamison. *Wooden: A Lifetime of Observations and Reflections on and off the Court.* Chicago, Ill.: Contemporary Books, 1997.

Woff, Richard. *The Ancient Greek Olympics.* London: Oxford University Press, 1999.

Young, David C. *The Modern Olympics: A Struggle for Revival.* Baltimore and London: Johns Hopkins University Press, 1996.

————. *The Olympic Myth of Greek Amateur Athletics.* Chicago: Ares Publishers, 1984.

INDEX

———— ✳ ————

QUEST BOOKS
are published by
The Theosophical Society in America
Wheaton, Illinois 60189-0270,
a worldwide, nonprofit membership organization
that promotes fellowship among all peoples of the world,
encourages the study of religion, philosophy, and science,
and supports spiritual growth and healing.

Today humanity is on the verge of becoming, for the first
time in its history, a global community. The only question is
what kind of community it will be. Quest Books strives to fulfill
the purpose of the Theosophical Society to act as a leavening;
to introduce into humanity a large mindedness, a freedom from
bias, an understanding of the values of the East and West; and
to point the way to human development as a means of service,
both for the individual and for the whole of humankind.

For more information about Quest Books,
visit **www.questbooks.net**
For more information about the Theosophical Society,
visit **www.theosophical.org**,
or contact **Olcott@theosmail.net**,
or (630) 668-1571.

*The Theosophical Publishing House is aided by
the generous support of the KERN FOUNDATION,
a trust dedicated to Theosophical education.*

ABOUT THE AUTHOR

A man of many enthusiasms, Phil Cousineau is a best-selling author, documentary filmmaker, photographer, adventure tour leader, and cultural historian who lectures around the world on a wide range of topics from mythology and creativity to architecture, art, and the movies. His many books include *Once and Future Myths: The Power of Ancient Stories in Modern Times*; *The Art of Pilgrimage: The Seeker's Guide to Making Travel Sacred*; *The Book of Roads: Travel Stories*; *Soul: An Archaeology: Readings from Socrates to Ray Charles*; *The Hero's Journey: Joseph Campbell on His Life and Work*; and most recently, *The Way Things Are: Conversations with Huston Smith on the Spiritual Life*.

Among his numerous screenwriting credits are *Ecological Design: Inventing the Future*; *Wayfinders: A Pacific Odyssey*; *The Peyote Road*; *The Hero's Journey: The World of Joseph Campbell*; the 1991 Academy Award-nominated *Forever Activists: Stories from the Abraham Lincoln Brigade*; and the newly released *A Seat at the Table: Struggling for American Indian Religious Freedom*.

He lives on Telegraph Hill in San Francisco, California, with Jo Beaton and their seven-year-old son, Jack.

Praise for Phil Cousineau's

———THE———

OLYMPIC
ODYSSEY

The Olympic Odyssey *showed me the remarkable spiritual foundation of the Games and their strong affinity with great religious ceremonies. It reveals how training for and competing in them is one of life's great and mythic journeys.*

—HUSTON SMITH, author of *The World's Religions,*
Why Religion Matters, and *The Way Things Are*

We *are much indebted for this beautiful book relighting the Olympic flame, the symbol that holds so much promise for overriding the divisive elements of color, race, creed, and belief in our fractured world.*

—ROBERT A. JOHNSON, author of *He, We, Inner Work,*
Transformation, and *Owning Your Own Shadow*

Phil's *unique genius is for helping us find the eternal dimensions of everyday life. Here is an exquisite revelation of the timeless hero's journey enacted by every Olympic athlete.*

—STEPHEN LARSEN, author of *The Mythic Imagination*
and *Fire in the Mind*